BIG-NOTE PIANO

the

Big Book of Children's Songs

ISBN 0-7935-0042-7

HAL•LEONARD®
CORPORATION
7777 W. BLUEMOUND RD. P.O. BOX 13819 MILWAUKEE, WI 53213

Visit Hal Leonard Online at
www.halleonard.com

Contents

ALOUETTE

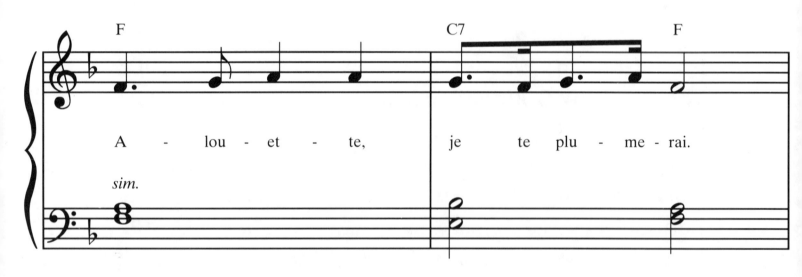

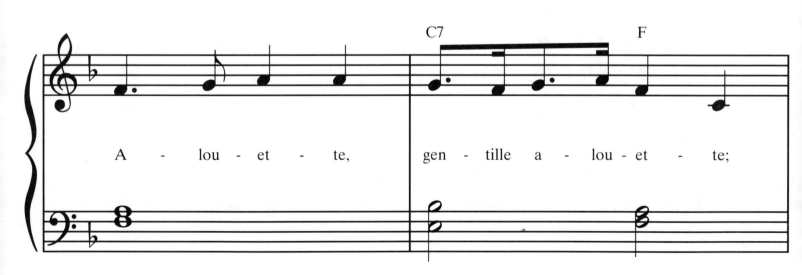

C7   F   *Fine*

A - lou - et - te, je te plu - me - rai.

F   C7   F

Je te plu - me - rai la têt'; je te plu - me - rai la têt'.

no chord   Repeat as needed*   *D.C. al Fine*

Et la têt', et la têt', A - lou - ett', a - lou - ett'.

*Each chorus adds a new part of the body, in reverse order. For example, Chorus 3 is sung:

Et le nez, et le nez,
Et le bec, et le bec,
Et la têt', et le têt',
Alouett', Alouett'.
Oh, etc.

2. le bec *(beak)*
3. le nez *(nose)*
4. les yeux *(eyes)*
5. le cou *(neck)*

6. les ailes *(wings)*
7. le dos *(back)*
8. les pattes *(feet)*
9. la queue *(tail)*

THE ALPHABET SONG

BIBBIDI-BOBBIDI-BOO

(From Walt Disney's "CINDERELLA")

Words by JERRY LIVINGSTON
Music by MACK DAVID and AL HOFFMAN

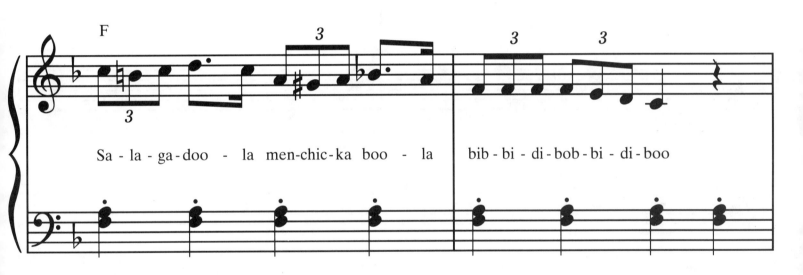

Sa - la - ga - doo - la men - chic - ka boo - la   bib - bi - di - bob - bi - di - boo

Put 'em to - geth - er and what have you got   bib - bi - di - bob - bi - di - boo.

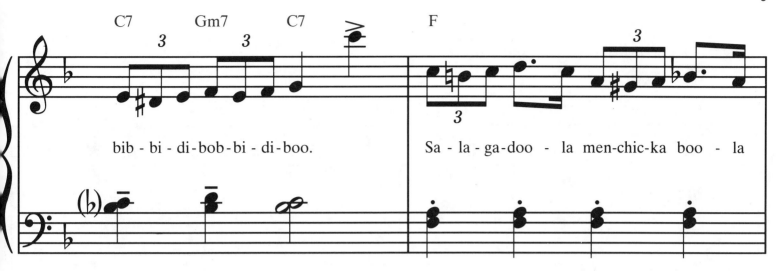

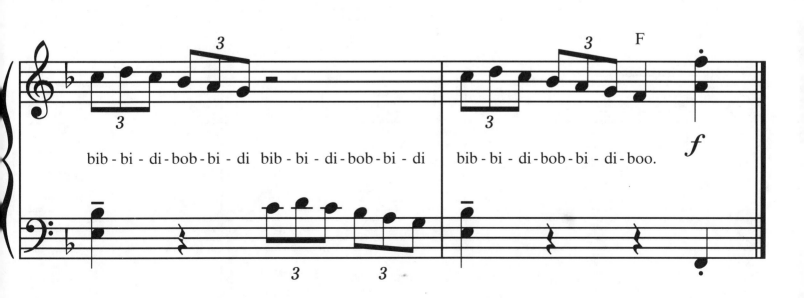

B-I-N-G-O

NOTE: Each time a letter of BINGO is deleted in the lyric, clap your hands in place of singing the letter.

THE BLUE-TAIL FLY
(JIMMY CRACK CORN)

When I was young, I used to wait up -

on old Mas - ter and pass his plate And fetch the bot - tle when

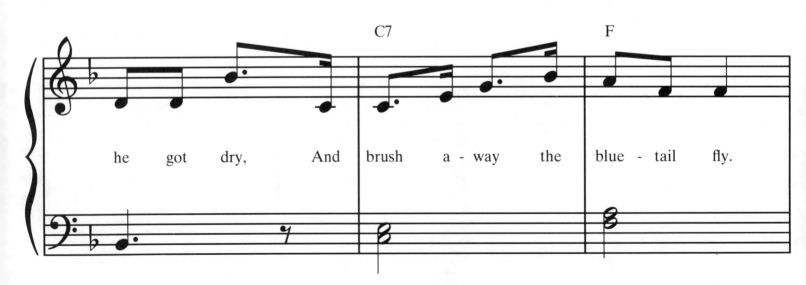

he got dry, And brush a - way the blue - tail fly.

Jim - mie crack corn, and I don't care,

Jim - mie crack corn and I don't care, Jim - mie crack corn and

I don't care, My Mas - ter's gone a - way.

Alternate Verses

2. And when he'd ride in the afternoon,
I'd follow with a hickory broom;
The pony being very shy,
Got bitten by a blue-tail fly.
Chorus:

3. One day he rode around the farm,
The flies so numerous, they did swarm,
One chanced to bite him on the thigh,
The devil take the blue-tail fly.
Chorus:

4. The pony run, he jump, he pitch,
He threw old Master in a ditch;
He died and the jury wondered why
The verdict was the blue-tail fly.
Chorus:

5. They laid him under a 'simmon tree,
His epitaph is there to see;
"Beneath the earth I'm forced to lie,
A victim of the blue-tail fly."
Chorus:

2. We went riding one afternoon,
I followed with a hickory broom,
The pony being very shy,
Got bitten by a blue-tail fly.
Chorus:

3. The pony he did rear and pitch,
He threw old Master in a ditch;
The jury asked the reason why,
The verdict was the blue-tail fly.
Chorus:

4. So we laid old Master down to rest;
And on a stone this last request;
"Beneath the earth I'm forced to lie,
A victim of the blue-tail fly."
Chorus:

CAMPTOWN RACES

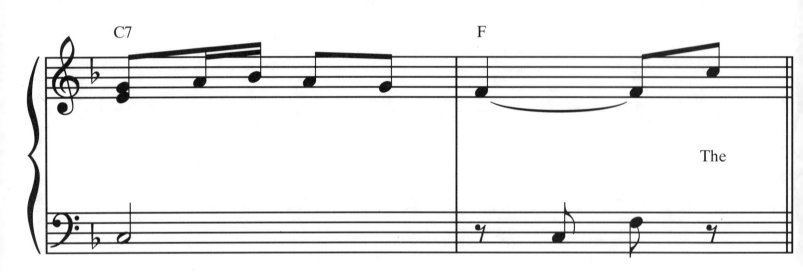

The

Camp - town   la - dies   sing   their   song,   Doo - dah,
long - tail   filly   and the   big   black   horse,   Doo - dah,

CLEMENTINE

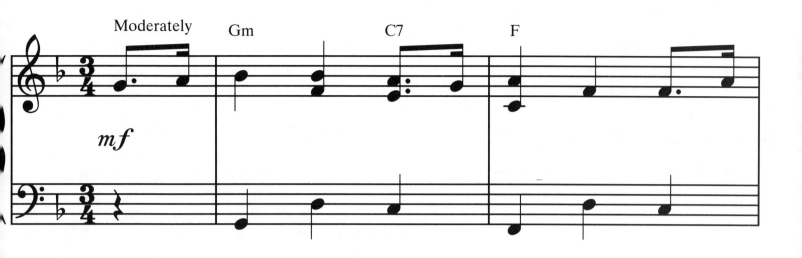

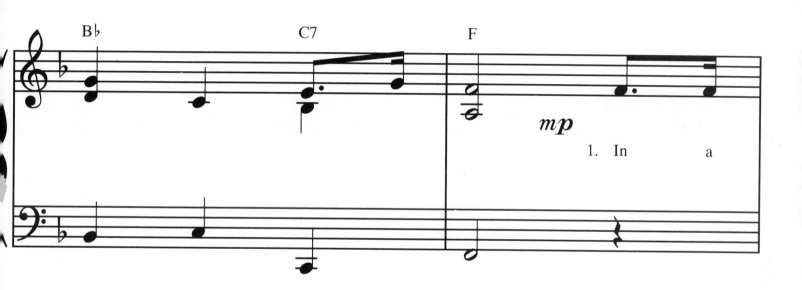

1. In a

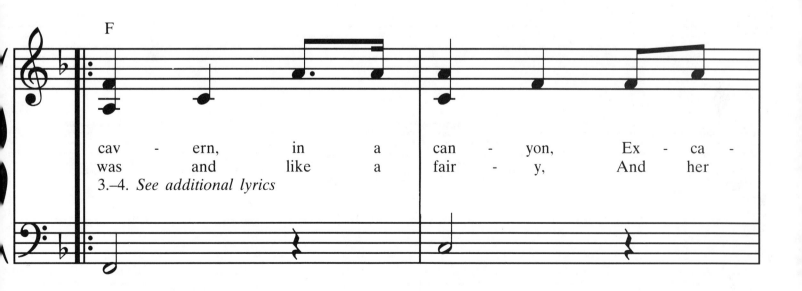

cav - ern, in a can - yon, Ex - ca -
was and like a fair - y, And her

3.–4. See additional lyrics

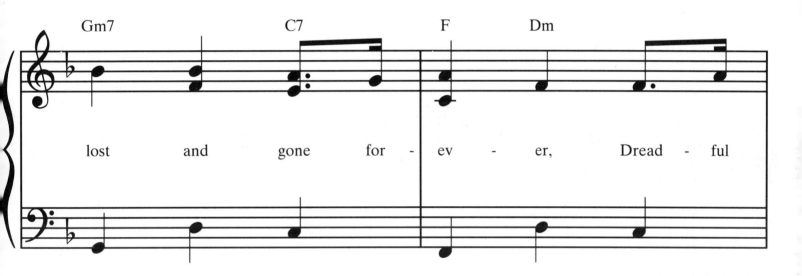

Additional lyrics

3. Drove she ducklings to the water
   Ev'ry morning just at nine,
   Hit her foot against a splinter,
   Fell into the foaming brine.

4. Ruby lips above the water
   Blowing bubbles soft and fine,
   But, alas, I was no swimmer,
   So I lost my Clementine.

CHIM, CHIM, CHER-EE

(From Walt Disney's "MARY POPPINS")

Words and Music by RICHARD M. SHERMAN
and ROBERT B. SHERMAN

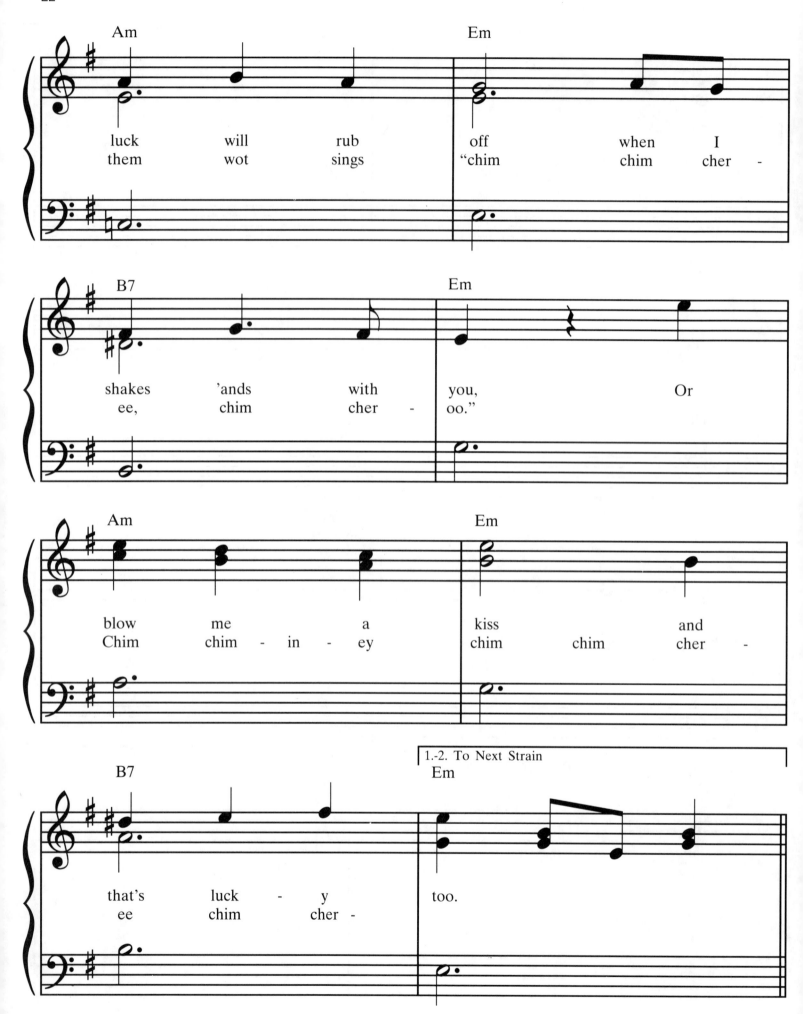

3.

B7

Fine

oo!

Em

B7

Em

B+

Now,   as   the   lad - der   of
I   choose   me   bris - tles   with

Em7

A

life   'as   been   strung,   You
pride,   yes,   I   do: A

DO-RE-MI

(From "THE SOUND OF MUSIC")

Words and Music by RICHARD M. SHERMAN
and ROBERT B. SHERMAN

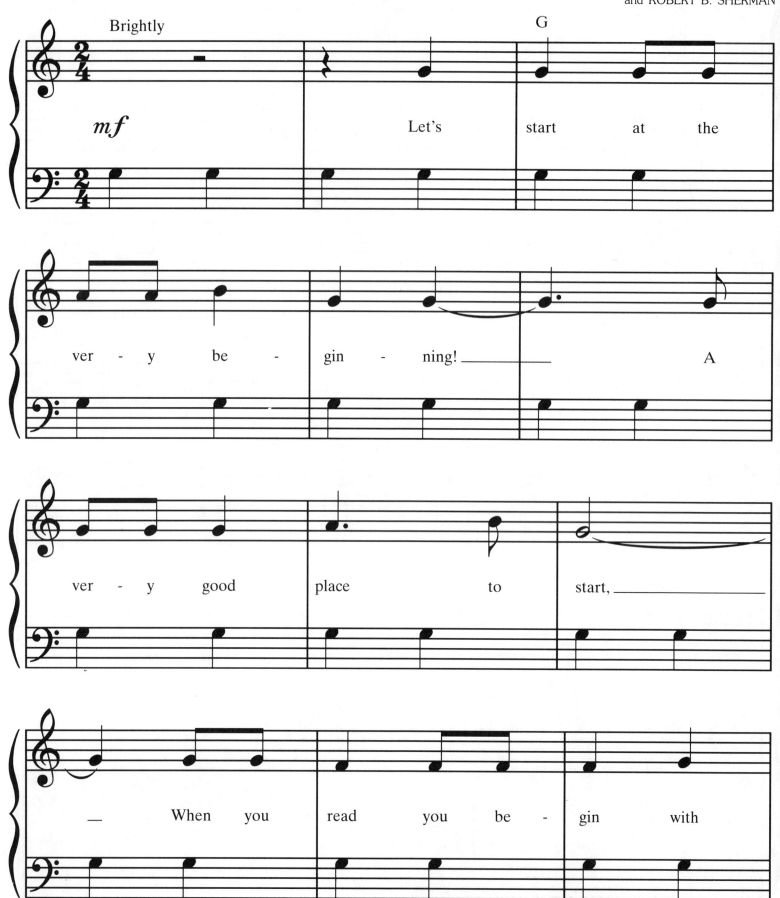

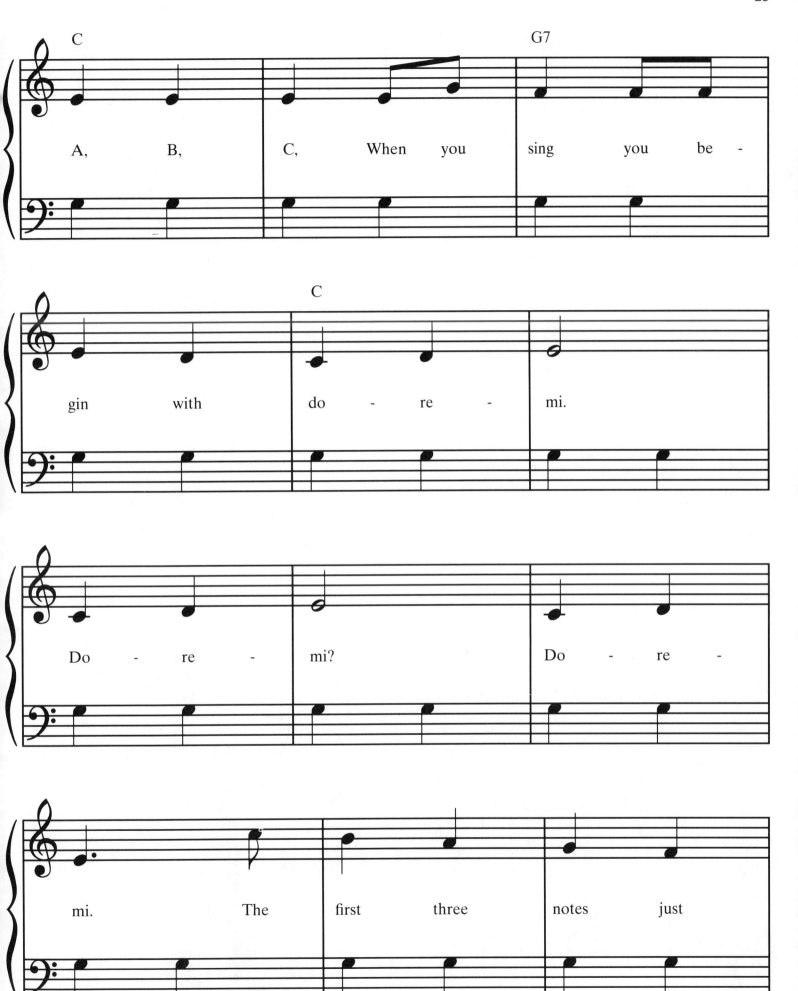

32

A DREAM IS A WISH YOUR HEART MAKES

(From Walt Disney's "CINDERELLA")

Words and Music by MACK DAVID,
AL HOFFMAN and JERRY LIVINGSTON

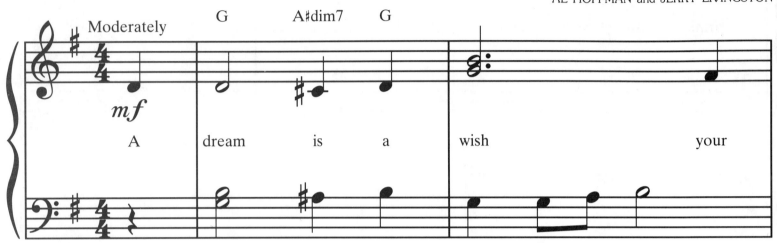

A dream is a wish your

heart makes _____ When you're

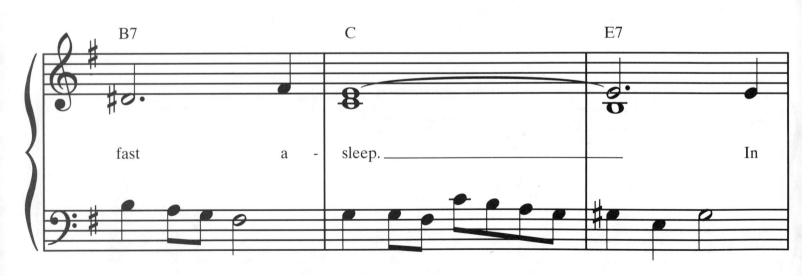

fast a - sleep. _____ In

THE FARMER IN THE DELL

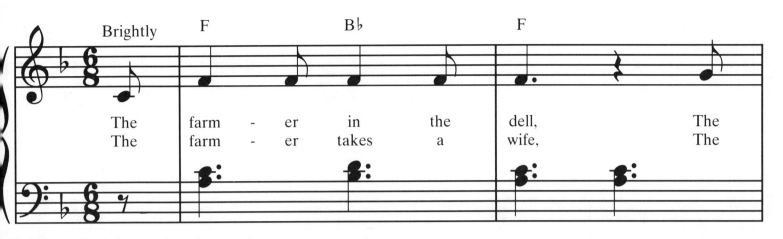

The farm - er in the dell, The
The farm - er takes a wife, The

farm - er in the dell, Heigh - o, the
farm - er takes a wife, Heigh - o, the

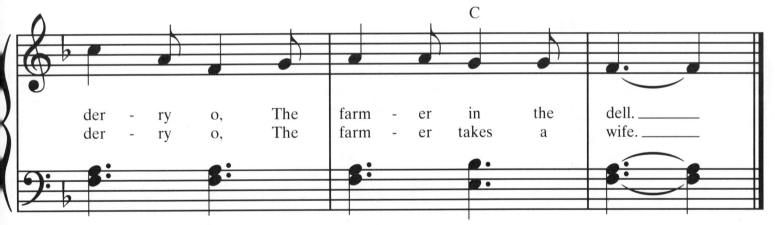

der - ry o, The farm - er in the dell._____
der - ry o, The farm - er takes a wife._____

3. The wife takes a child, etc.

4. The child takes a nurse, etc.

5. The nurse takes a dog, etc.

6. The dog takes a cat, etc.

7. The cat takes a rat, etc.

8. The rat takes the cheese, etc.

9. The cheese stands alone, etc.

EENSY WEENSY SPIDER

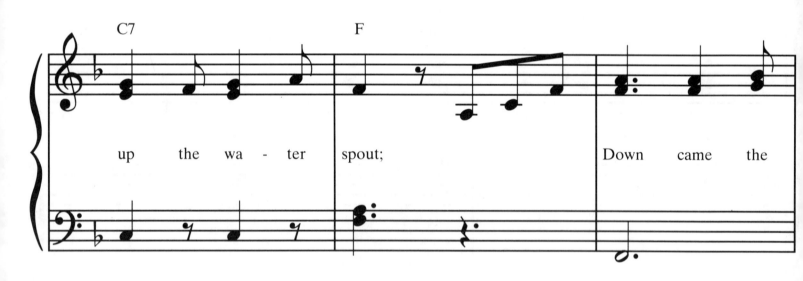

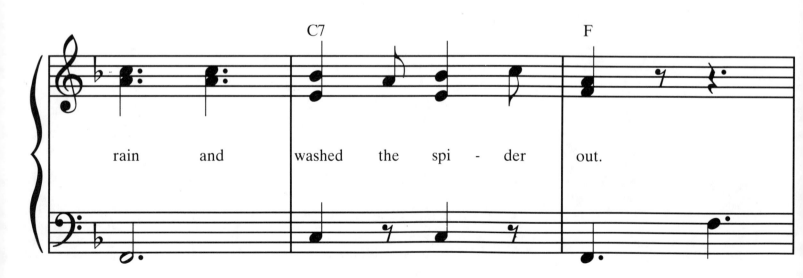

FRÈRE JACQUES
(ARE YOU SLEEPING)

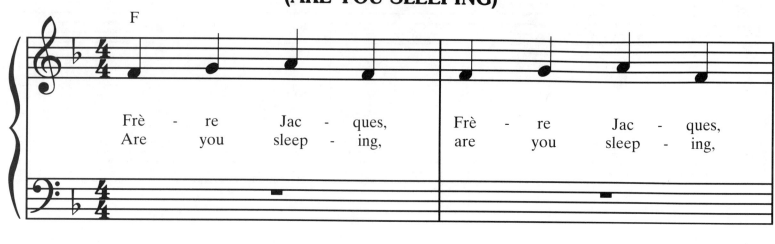

Frè - re Jac - ques, Frè - re Jac - ques,
Are you sleep - ing, are you sleep - ing,

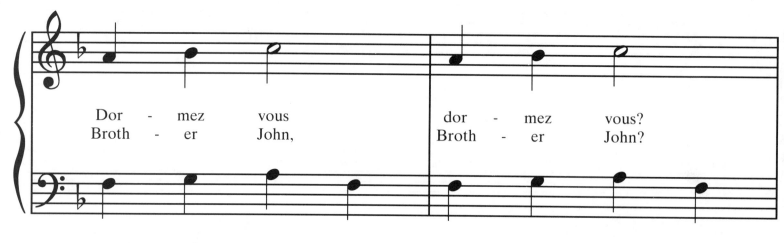

Dor - mez vous dor - mez vous?
Broth - er John, Broth - er John?

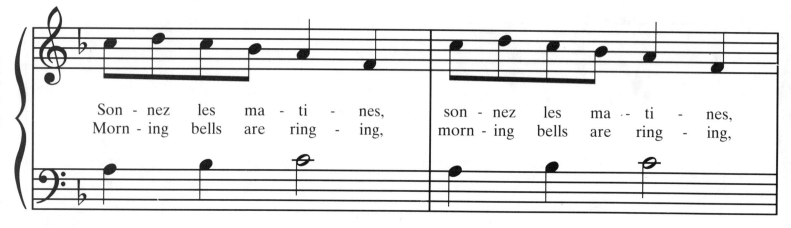

Son - nez les ma - ti - nes, son - nez les ma - ti - nes,
Morn - ing bells are ring - ing, morn - ing bells are ring - ing,

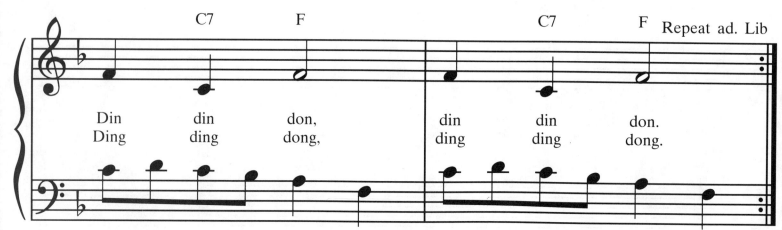

Din din don, din din don.
Ding din ding dong, ding din ding dong.

HICKORY DICKORY DOCK

FROSTY THE SNOW MAN

Words and Music by STEVE NELSON
and JACK ROLLINS

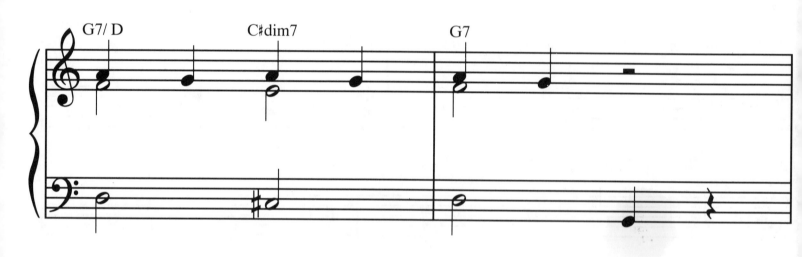

Frost - y the snow man was a
Frost - y the snow man knew the

jol - ly hap - py soul, With a
sun was hot that day, So he

corn cob pipe and a but - ton nose ___ and two
said "Let's run and we'll have some fun ___ now be -

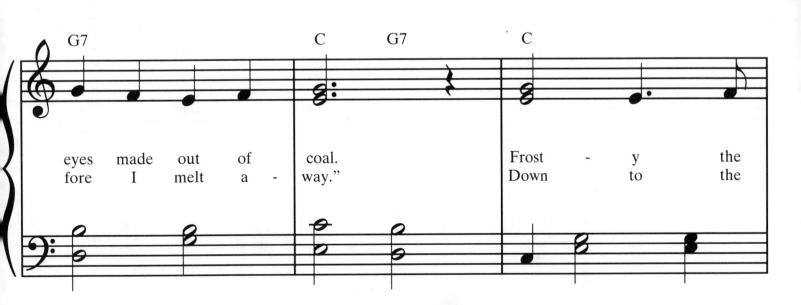

eyes made out of coal. Frost - y the
fore I melt a - way." Down to the

45

snow man was a - live as he could
snow man had to hur - ry on his

be, And the chil - dren say he could
way, But he waved good - bye say - in',

laugh and play ___ just the same as you and
"Don't you cry, ___ I'll be back a - gain some -

1.
me.

2.
day."

Thump - et - y thump thump, thump - et - y thump thump,

G7

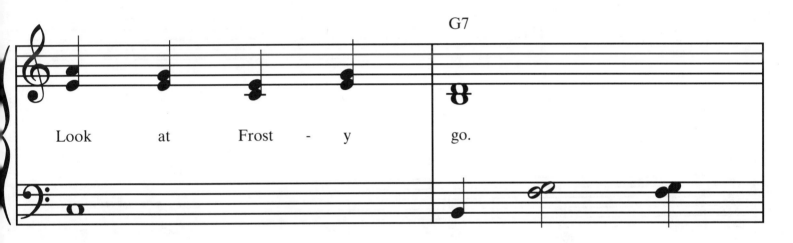

Look at Frost - y go.

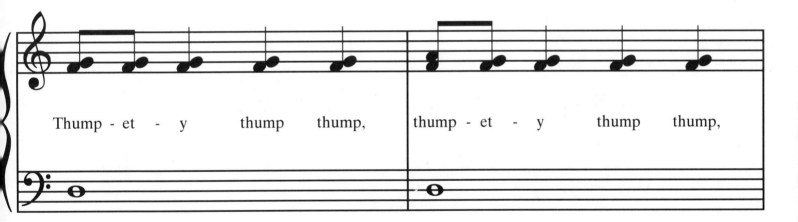

Thump - et - y thump thump, thump - et - y thump thump,

C

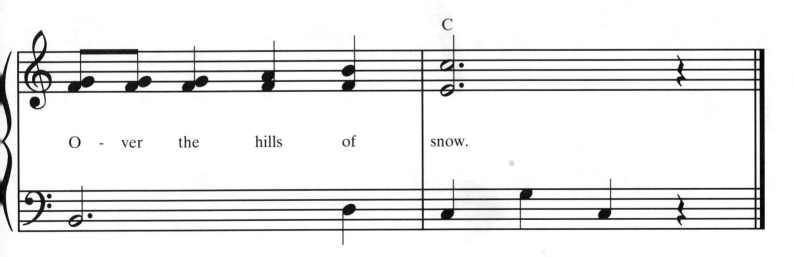

O - ver the hills of snow.

HAPPY BIRTHDAY TO YOU

Words and Music by MILDRED J. HILL
and PATTY S. HILL

49

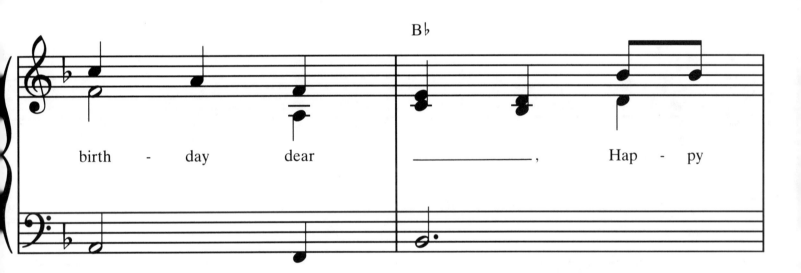

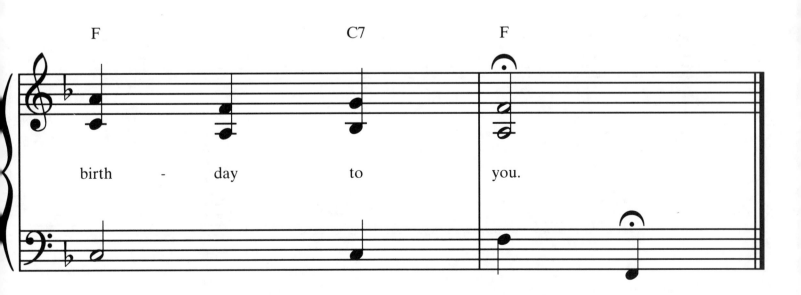

HEY, DIDDLE, DIDDLE

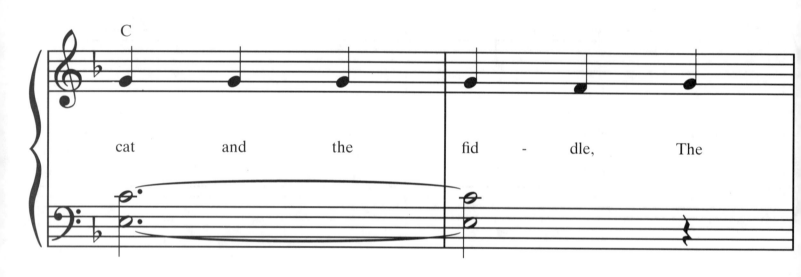

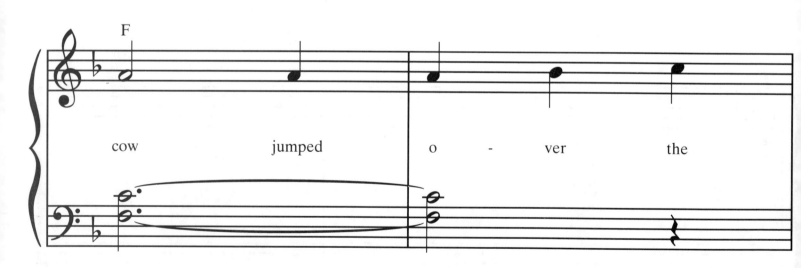

HUMPTY DUMPTY

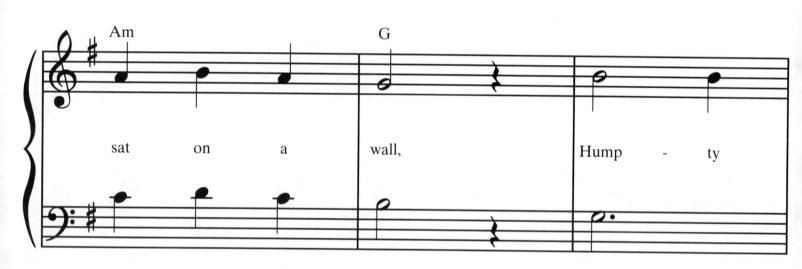

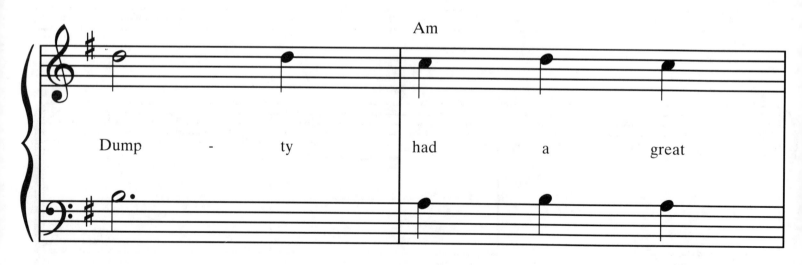

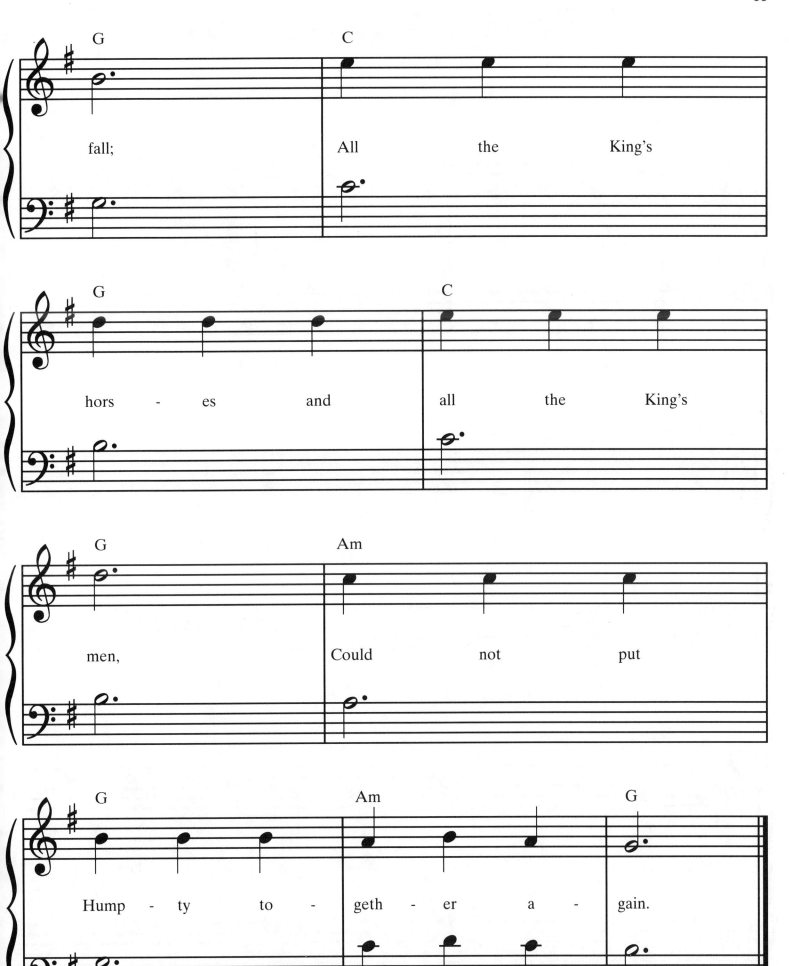

I WHISTLE A HAPPY TUNE

(From "THE KING AND I")

Lyrics by OSCAR HAMMERSTEIN II
Music by RICHARD RODGERS

Moderately

When ev - er I feel a - fraid I

hold my head e - rect And whis - tle a hap - py

tune and ev - 'ry sin - gle time The

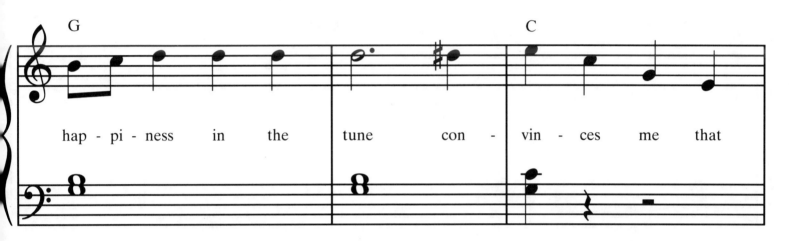

hap - pi - ness in the tune con - vin - ces me that

I'm not a - fraid._____ Make be - lieve you're

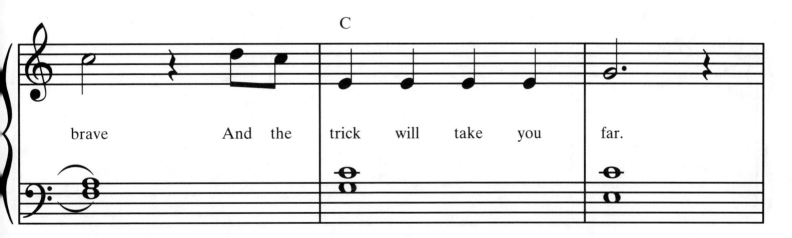

brave And the trick will take you far.

You may be as brave as ya make be - lieve you are.

(whistle) _____

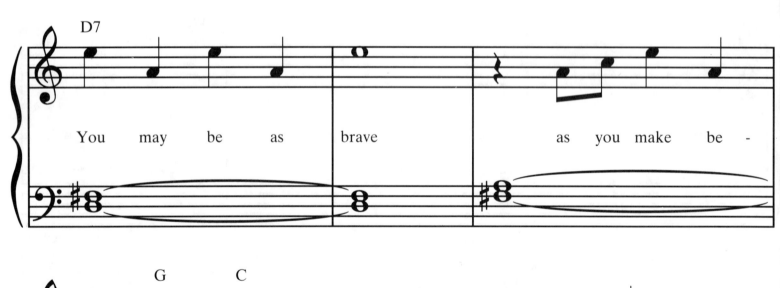

You may be as brave as you make be -

lieve you are.

I'VE BEEN WORKING ON THE RAILROAD

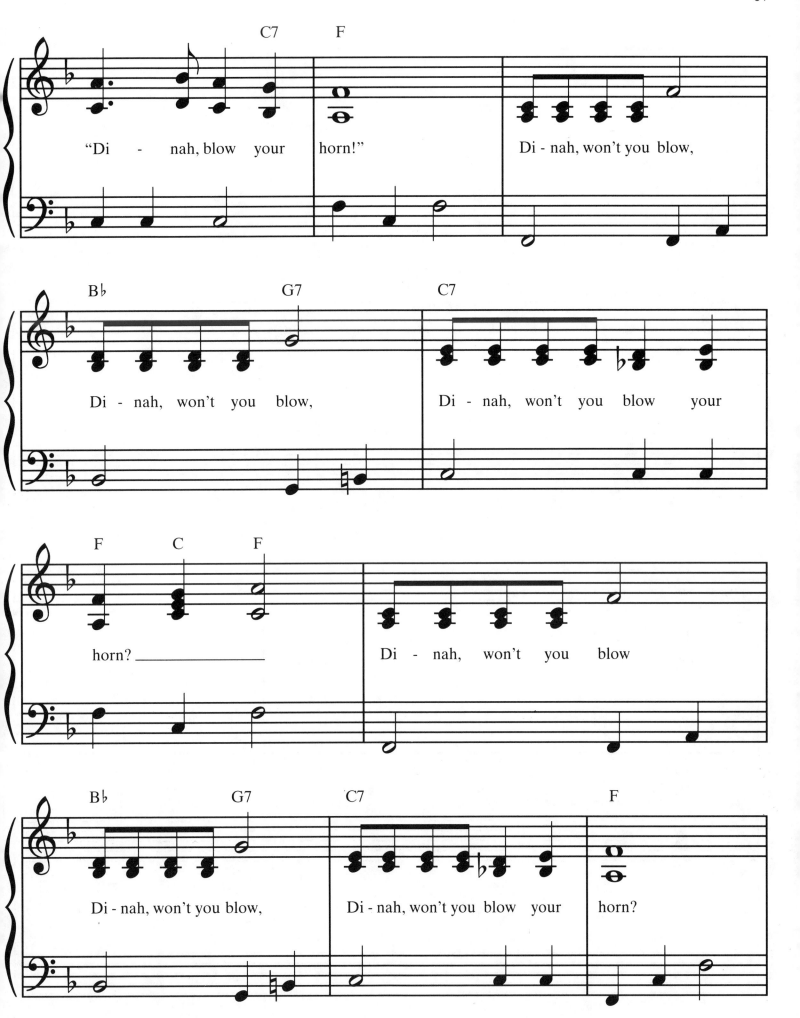

IT'S A SMALL WORLD

March Tempo

Words and Music by Richard M. Sherman and Robert B. Sherman

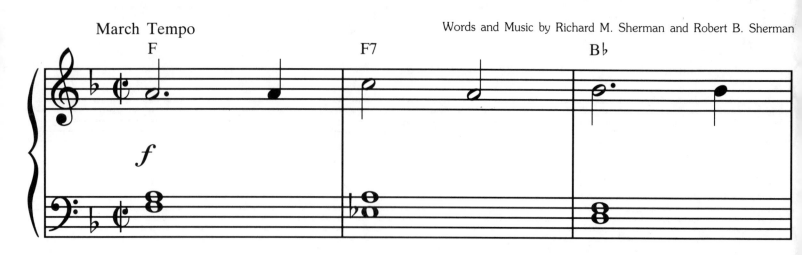

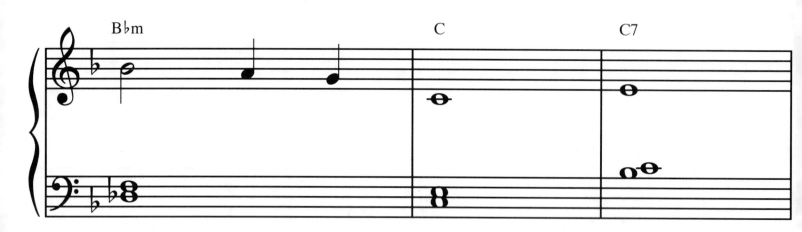

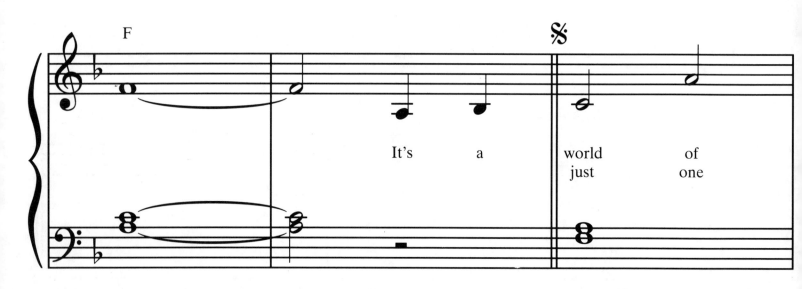

It's a world of just one

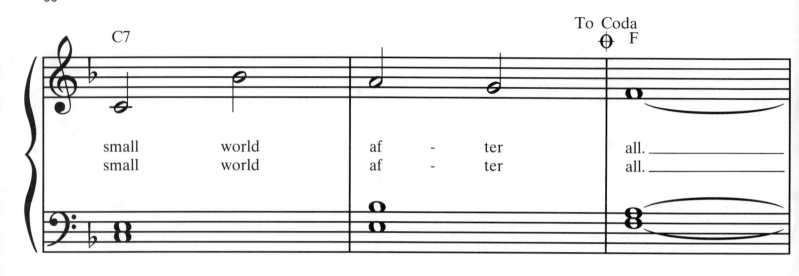

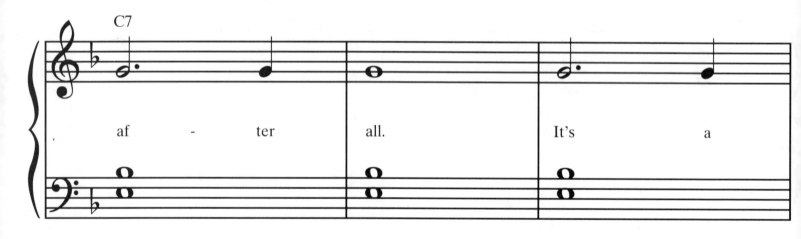

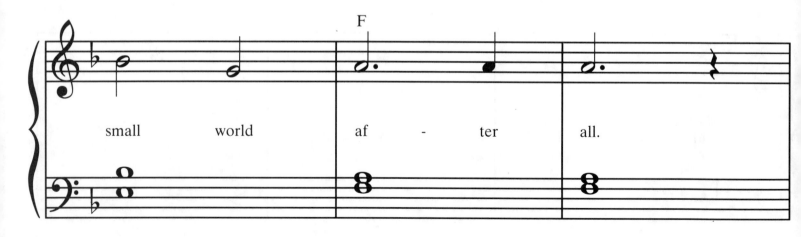

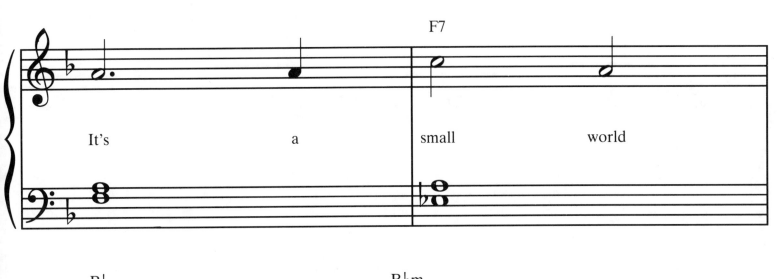

It's   a   small   world

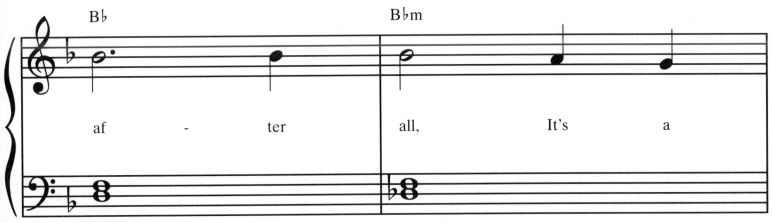

af - ter   all,   It's   a

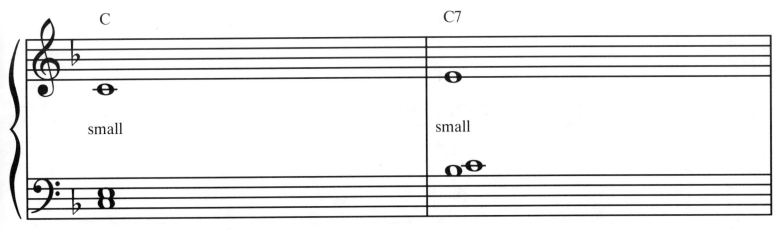

small   small

world. _____   There   is

all.

JACK AND JILL

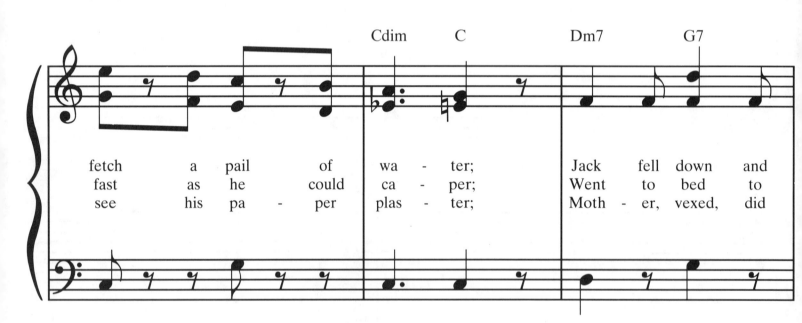

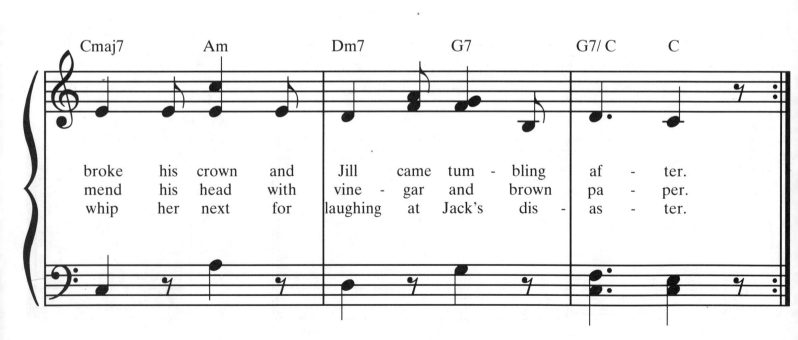

Jack and Jill went up the hill to
Up Jack got and went and home did trot as
Jill came in and and she did grin to

fetch a pail of wa - ter; Jack fell down and
fast as he could ca - per; Went to bed to
see his pa - per plas - ter; Moth - er, vexed, did

broke his crown and Jill came tum - bling af - ter.
mend his head with vine - gar and brown pa - per.
whip her next for laughing at Jack's dis - as - ter.

JOHN JACOB JINGLEHEIMER SCHMIDT

LAVENDER BLUE

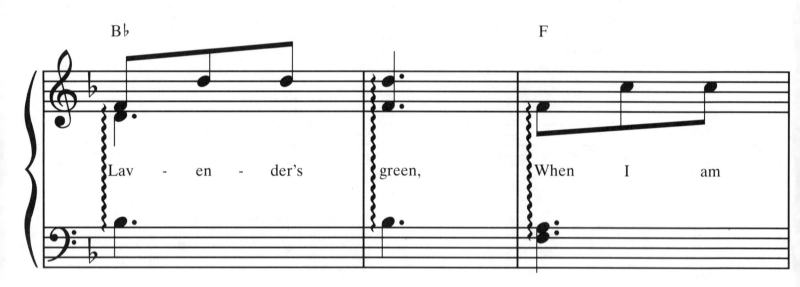

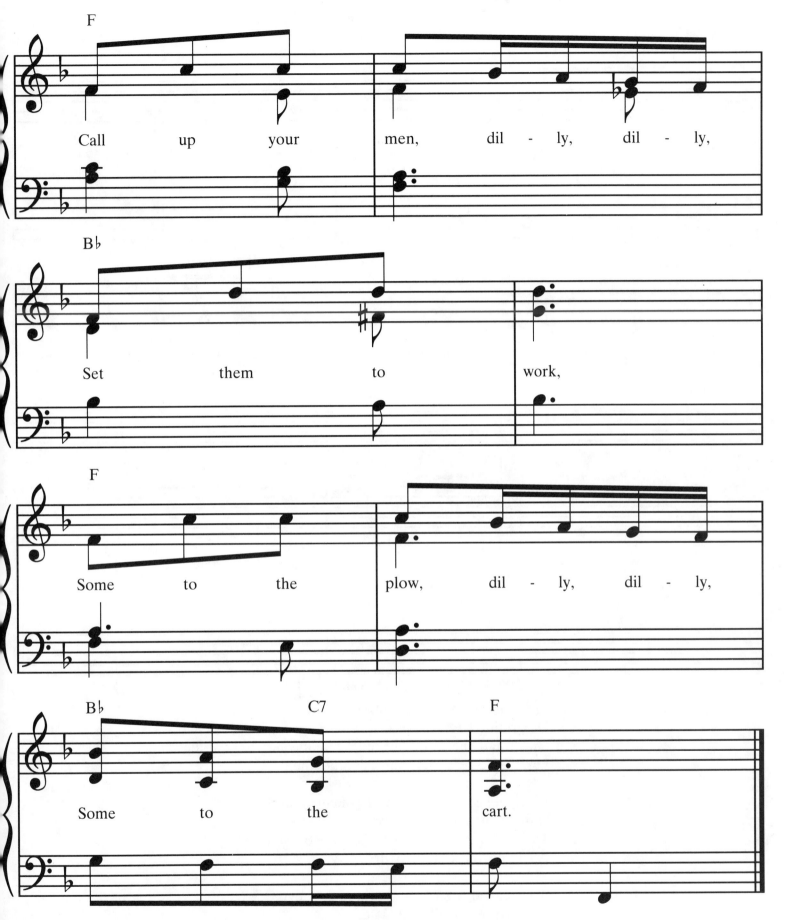

Some to make hay, dilly, dilly,
Some to cut corn,
While you and I, dilly, dilly,
Keep ourselves warm.

LITTLE BO-PEEP

3. Then up she took her little crook,
Determined for to find them;
She found them indeed, but it made her heart bleed,
For they'd left their tails behind them.

4. It happened one day, as Bo-Peep did stray
Unto a meadow hard by;
There she espied their tails, side by side,
All hung on a tree to dry.

5. She heaved a sigh, and wiped her eye,
And ran o'er hill and dale,
And tried what she could, as a shepherdess should,
To tack each sheep to its tail.

LITTLE BOY BLUE

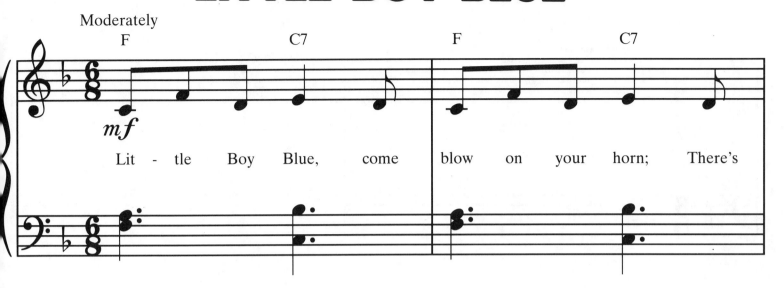

LITTLE MISS MUFFET

Lit - tle Miss Muf - fet sat on a tuf - fet,

eat - ing some curds and whey. _____ There

came a big Spi - der and sat down be - side her, and

fright - ened Miss Muf - fet a - way. _____

LONDON BRIDGE

3. Iron bars will bend and break,
   Bend and break, bend and break;
   Iron bars will bend and break,
   My fair lady.

4. Build it up with gold and silver,
   Gold and silver, gold and silver;
   Build it up with gold and silver,
   My fair lady.

MICKEY MOUSE MARCH

(From Walt Disney's "THE MICKEY MOUSE CLUB")

Bright march tempo

Words and Music by JIMMIE DODD

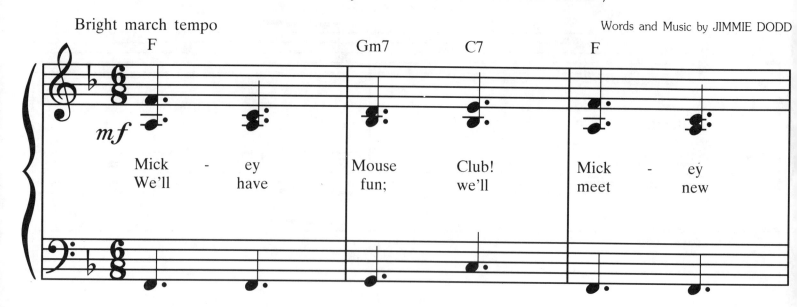

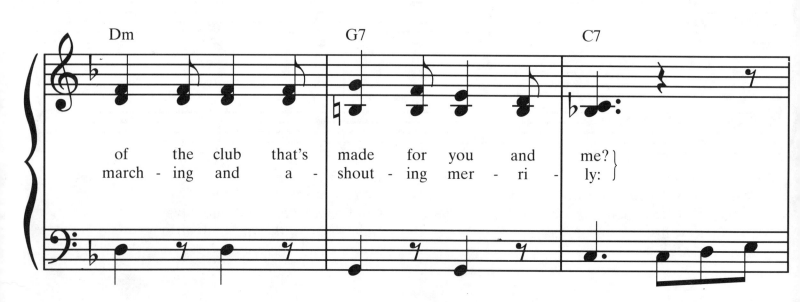

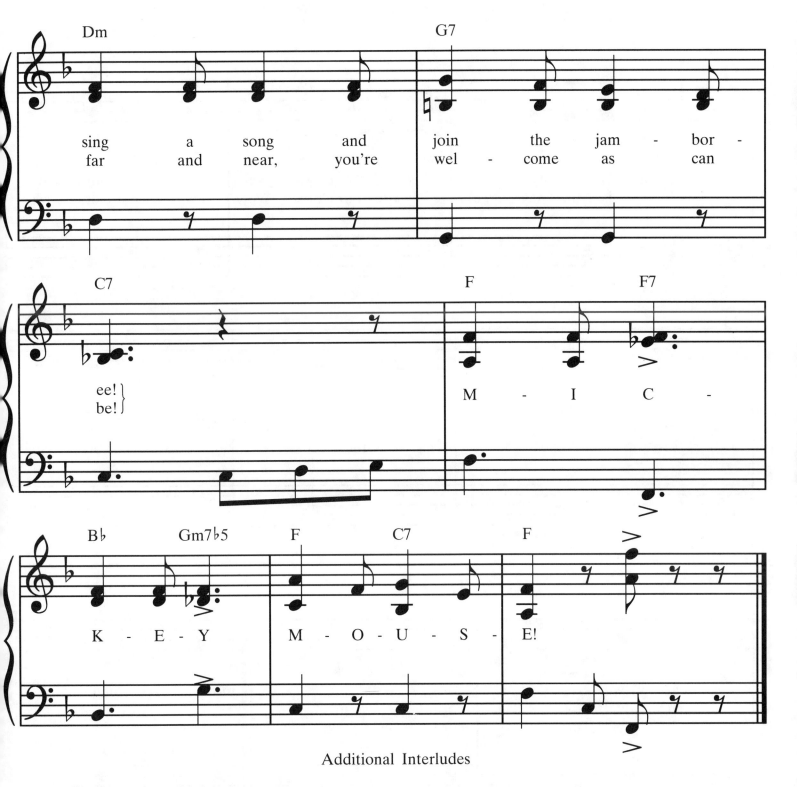

Additional Interludes

3. We'll do things and we'll go places!

4. All around the world we're marching!

5. We have fun and we play safely!

6. Look both ways when you cross crossings!

7. Don't take chances! Play with safety!

8. When you ride your bike be careful!

9. Play a little, work a little.

10. Sing a song while you are working!

11. It will make your burden lighter.

12. Do a good turn for your neighbor.

13. You can learn things while you're playing.

14. It's a lot of fun to learn things.

THE MULBERRY BUSH

4. This is the way we scrub the floor, *etc.*
So early Wednesday morning.

5. This is the way we mend our clothes, *etc.*
So early Thursday morning.

6. This is the way we sweep the house, *etc.*
So early Friday morning.

7. This is the way we bake our bread, *etc.*
So early Saturday morning.

8. This is the way we go to church, *etc.*
So early Sunday morning.

OH WHERE, OH WHERE HAS MY LITTLE DOG GONE?

MY FAVORITE THINGS

(From "THE SOUND OF MUSIC")

Lyrics by OSCAR HAMMERSTEIN II
Music by RICHARD RODGERS

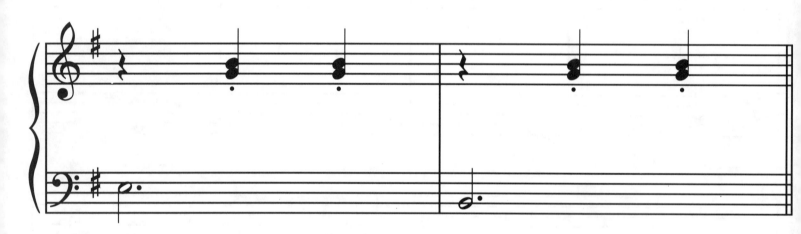

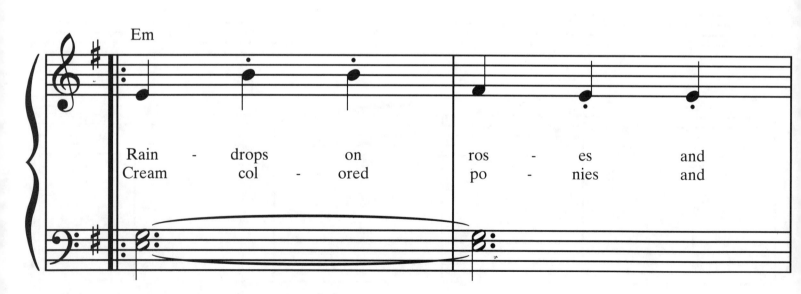

Rain - drops on ros - es and
Cream col - ored po - nies and

whisk - ers on kit - tens; Bright cop - per
crisp ap - ple stru - dels; Door - bells and

ket - tles and warm wool - en mit - tens;
sleigh - bells and schnitz - el with noo - dles;

Brown pa - per pack - ag - es
Wild geese that fly with the

tied up with strings, } These are a
moon on their wings, }

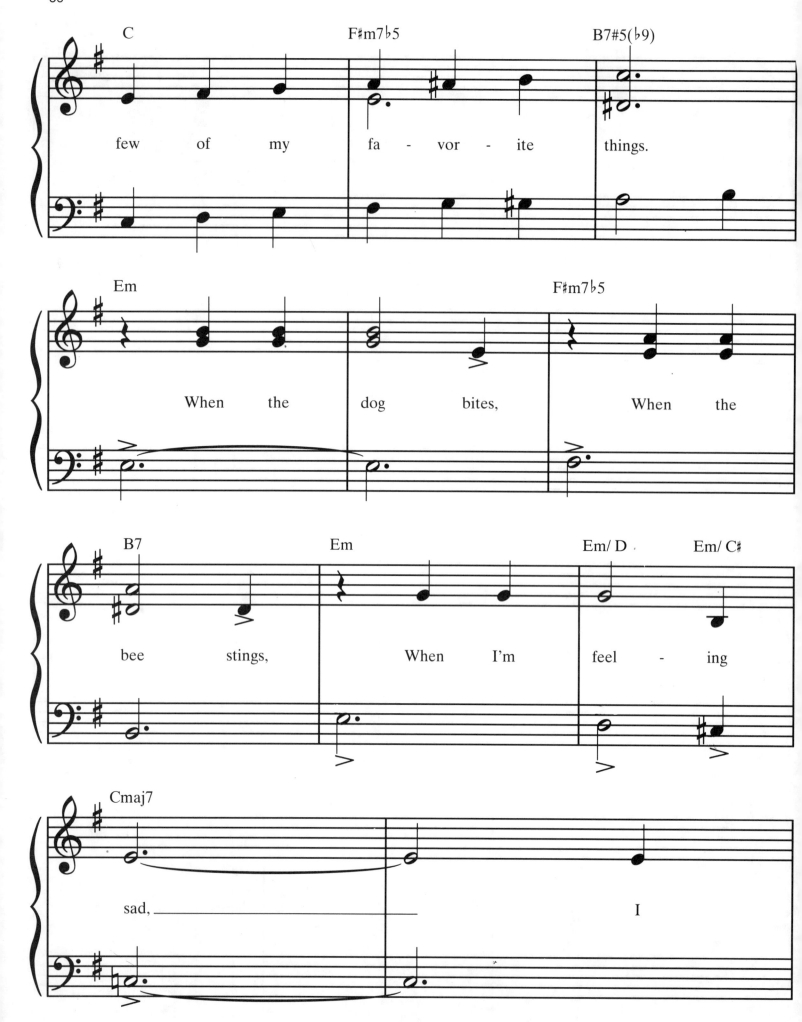

OH! SUSANNA

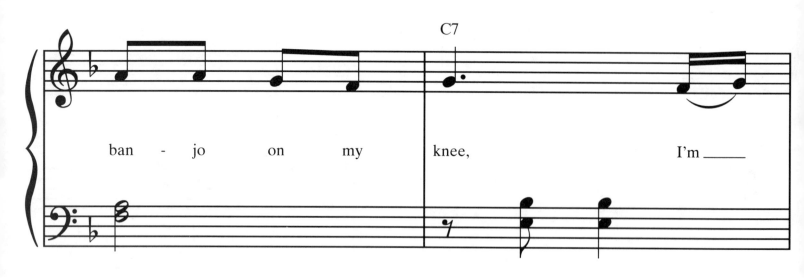

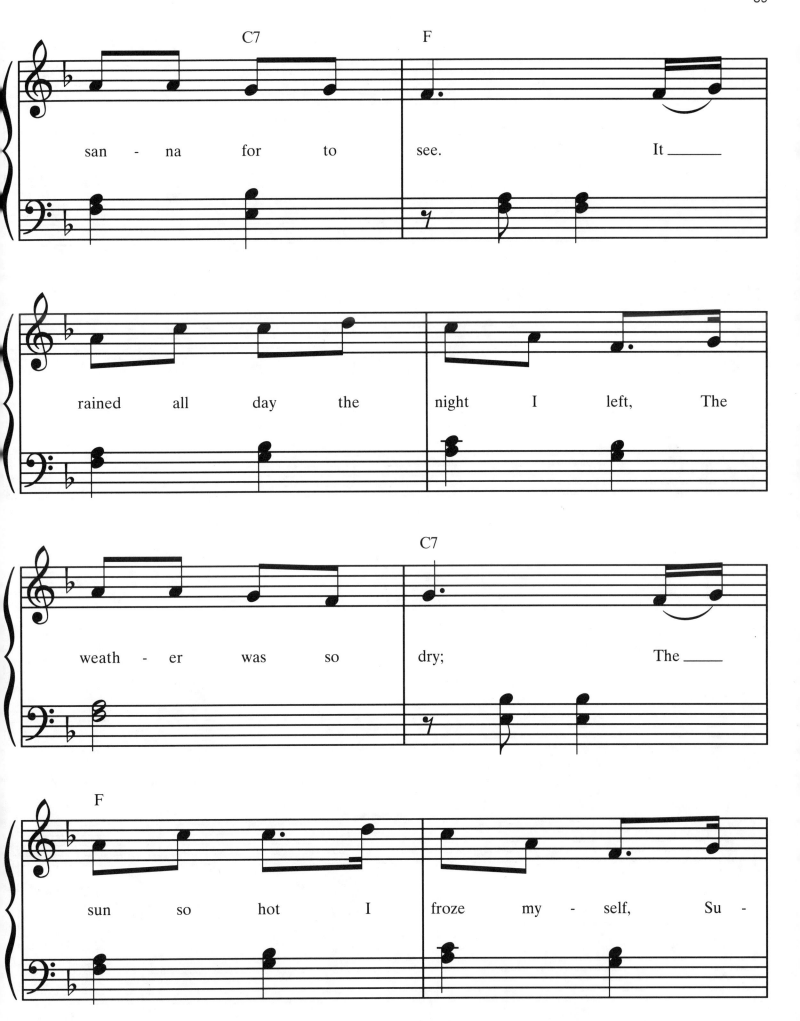

PETER COTTONTAIL

Words and Music by STEVE NELSON
and JACK ROLLINS

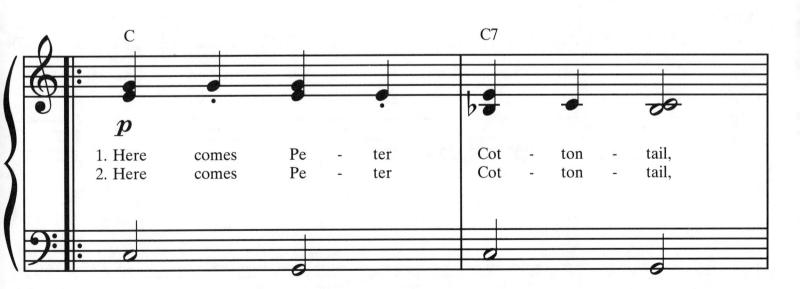

1. Here comes Pe - ter Cot - ton - tail,
2. Here comes Pe - ter Cot - ton - tail,

bun - ny trail, _____
bun - ny trail, _____

Hip - pi - ty hop - pi - ty
Hip - pi - ty hop - pi - ty

Hap - py Eas - ter
Hap - py Eas - ter

Day.

Day.

Year-'Round Version:

1. Look at Peter Cottontail,
   Hoppin' down the bunny trail,
   A rabbit of distinction so they say.
   He's the king of Bunny land,
   'Cause his eyes are shiny and
   He can spot the wolf a mile away.
   When the others go for clover
   And the big bad wolf appears
   He's the one that's watching over
   Givin' signals with his ears.
   And that's why folks in Rabbit town
   Feel so free when he's aroun'
   Peter's helpin' someone ev'ry day.

2. Little Peter Cottontail,
   Hoppin' down the bunny trail,
   Happened to stop for carrots on the way.
   Something told him it was wrong,
   Farmer Jones might come along
   And an awful price he'd have to pay.
   But he knew his legs were faster
   So he nibbled three or four
   And he almost met disaster
   When he heard that shot gun roar.
   Oh, that's how Peter Cottontail
   Hop-pin' down the bunny trail
   Lost his tail but still he got away.

THE OLD GRAY MARE

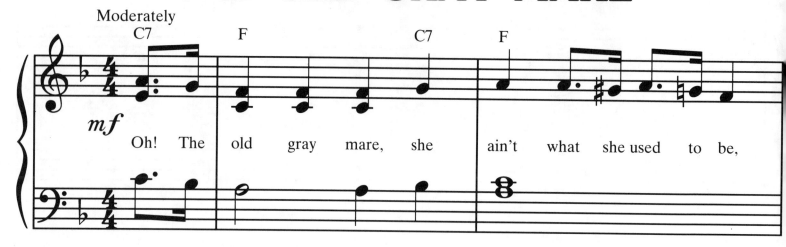

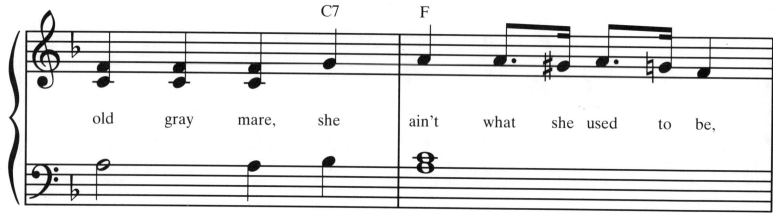

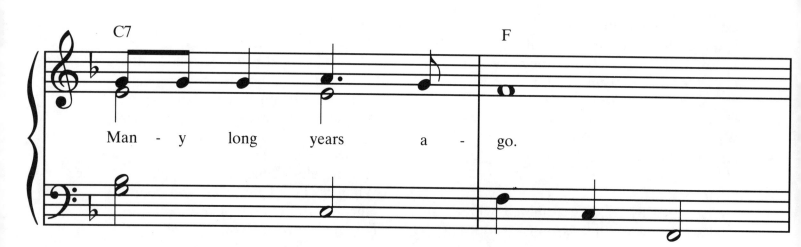

OLD KING COLE

Old King Cole was a mer-ry old __ soul, and a mer-ry old soul was

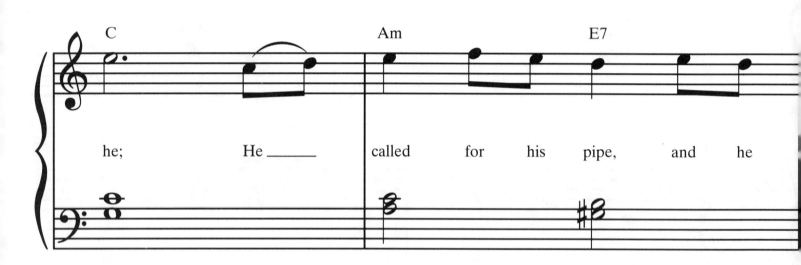

he; He __ called for his pipe, and he

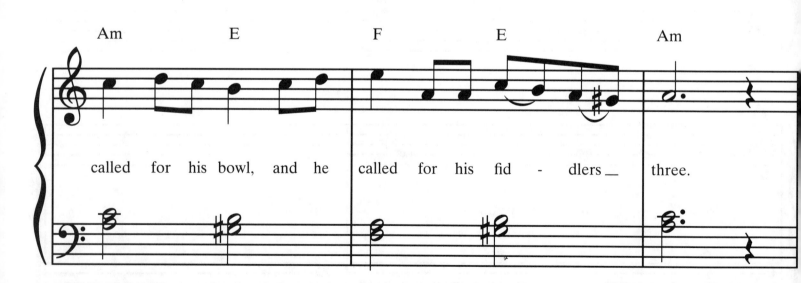

called for his bowl, and he called for his fid - dlers __ three.

OLD MacDONALD HAD A FARM

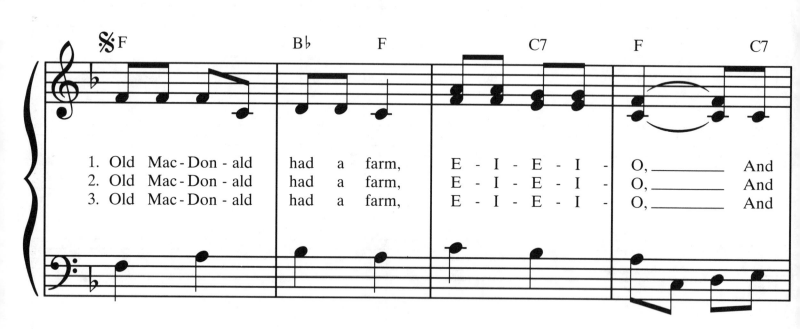

1. Old Mac-Don-ald had a farm, E - I - E - I - O, _____ And
2. Old Mac-Don-ald had a farm, E - I - E - I - O, _____ And
3. Old Mac-Don-ald had a farm, E - I - E - I - O, _____ And

on his farm he had a cow, E - I - E - I - O. _____ With a
on his farm he had a pig, E - I - E - I - O. _____ With an
on his farm he had a duck, E - I - E - I - O. _____ With a

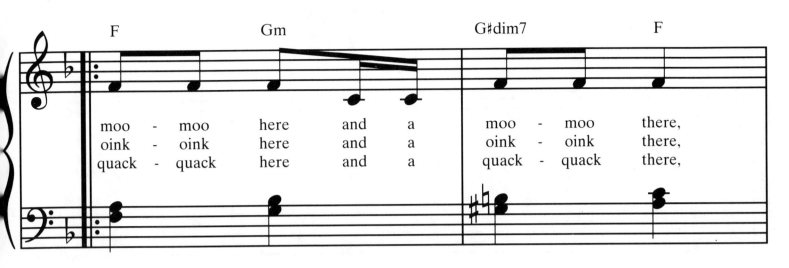

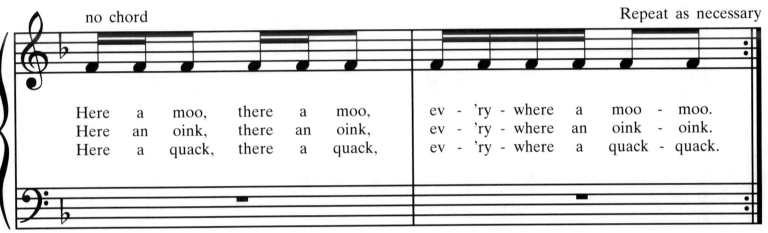

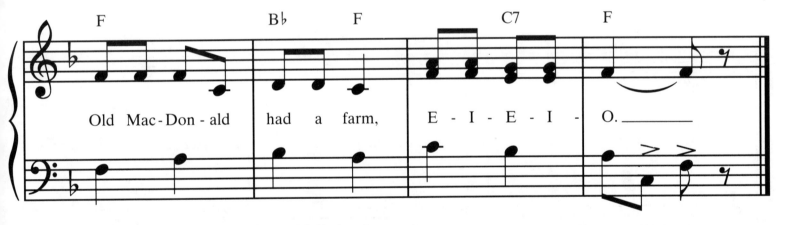

4. Old MacDonald had a farm,
E-I-E-I-O,
And on his farm he had a horse,
E-I-E-I-O.
With a neigh-neigh here and a neigh-neigh there, etc.

5. Old MacDonald had a farm,
E-I-E-I-O,
And on his farm he had a donkey,
E-I-E-I-O.
With a hee-haw here, etc.

6. Old MacDonald had a farm,
E-I-E-I-O,
And on his farm he had some chickens,
E-I-E-I-O.
With a chick-chick here, etc.

For additional verses, add your own animals.

ON TOP OF OLD SMOKY

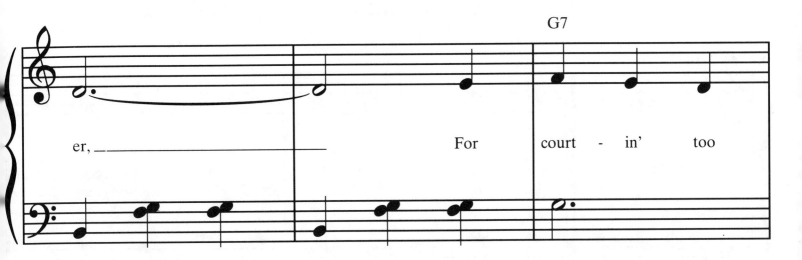

er, _____ For court - in' too

slow. _____ 2. (see additional lyrics)

skies. _____

2. A-courtin's a pleasure,
    A-flirtin's a grief,
    A false-hearted lover
    Is worse than a thief.

3. For a thief, he will rob you,
    And take what you have,
    But a false-hearted lover
    Sends you to your grave.

4. She'll hug you and kiss you,
    And tell you more lies,
    Than the ties on the railroad,
    Or the stars in the skies.

POLLY WOLLY DOODLE

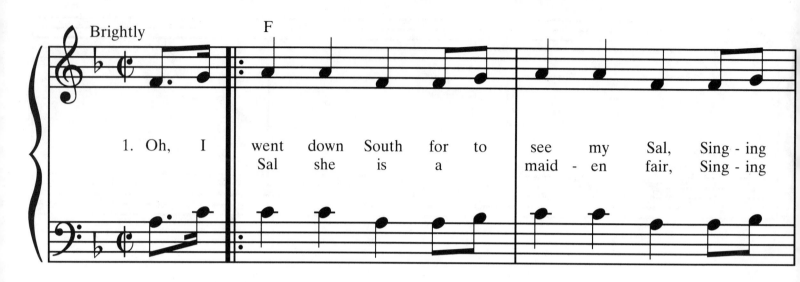

1. Oh, I went down South for to see my Sal, Sing-ing
Sal she is a maid-en fair, Sing-ing

pol-ly wol-ly doo-dle all the day. My __ Sal she is a
pol-ly wol-ly doo-dle all the day. With __ curl-y eyes and

spunk-y gal, Sing-ing pol-ly wol-ly doo-dle all the day. } Fare thee
laugh-ing hair, Sing-ing pol-ly wol-ly doo-dle all the day. }

well,   Fare thee   well,   Fare thee   well,   my   fair - y

fay.   For I'm   goin' to Lou'-si - an - a   for to   see my Su - zi - an - na Sing-ing

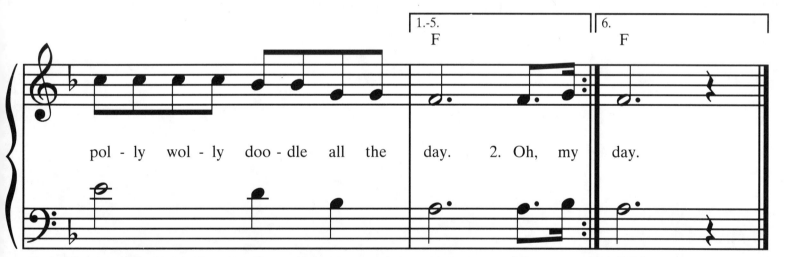

pol - ly wol - ly doo - dle all the   day.   2. Oh, my   day.

3. Oh, a grasshopper sittin' on a railroad track,
Singing polly-wolly-doodle all the day.
A pickin' his teeth with a carpet tack,
Singing polly-wolly-doodle all the day.
Chorus

4. Oh, I went to bed, but it wasn't no use,
Singing polly-wolly-doodle all the day.
My feet stuck out like a chicken roost,
Singing polly-wolly-doodle all the day.
Chorus

5. Behind the barn down on my knees,
Singing polly-wolly-doodle all the day.
I thought I heard a chicken sneeze,
Singing polly-wolly-doodle all the day.
Chorus

6. He sneezed so hard with the whooping cough,
Singing polly-wolly-doodle all the day.
He sneezed his head and tail right off,
Singing polly-wolly-doodle all the day.
Chorus

POP! GOES THE WEASEL

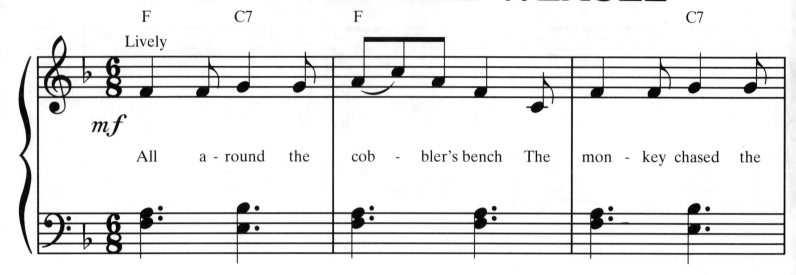

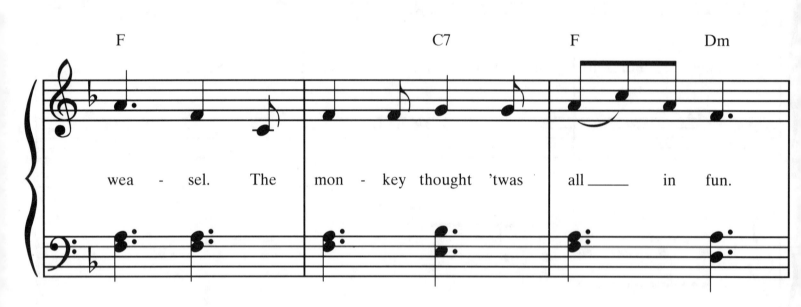

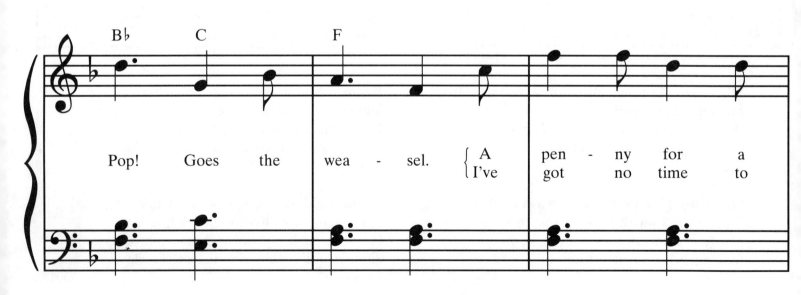

THE RAINBOW CONNECTION

By PAUL WILLIAMS
and KENNETH L. ASCHER

Moderately, with a Lilt

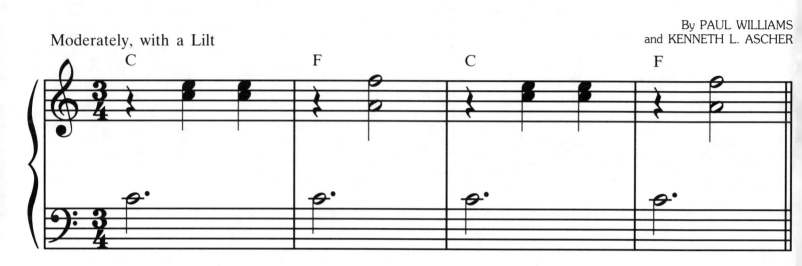

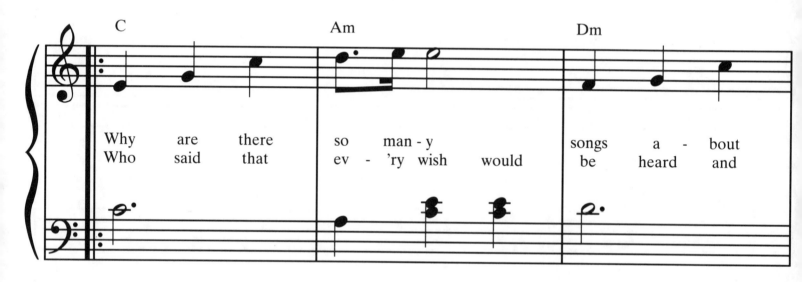

Why are there so man-y songs a-bout
Who said that ev-'ry wish would be heard and

rain-bows and what's on the oth - er
an-swered and when wished on the morn - ing

RED RIVER VALLEY

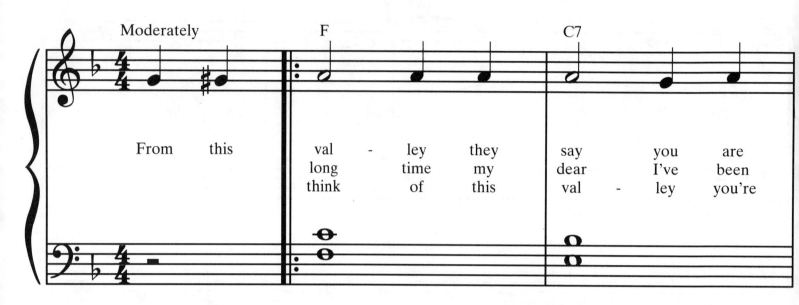

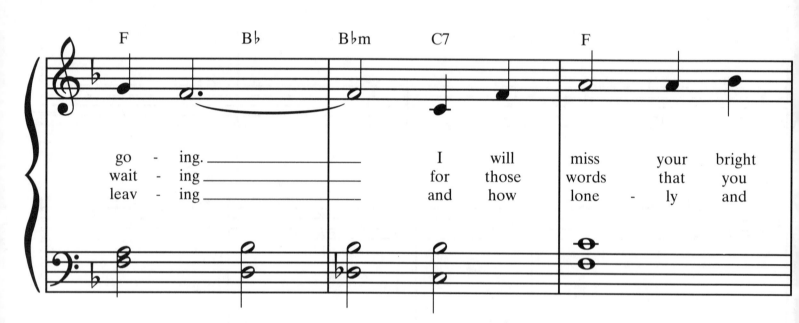

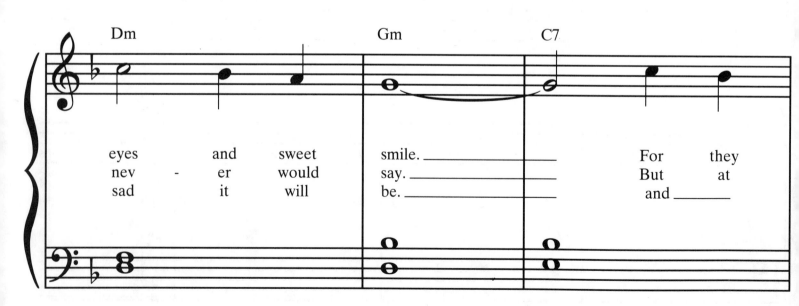

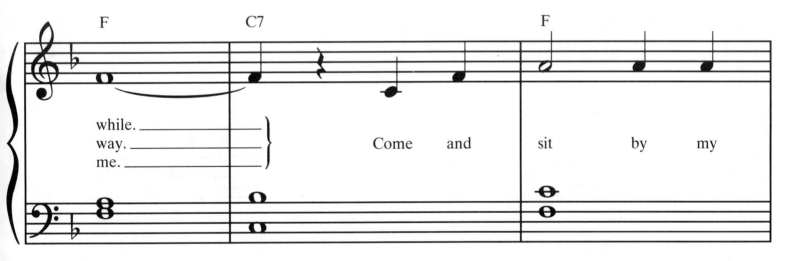

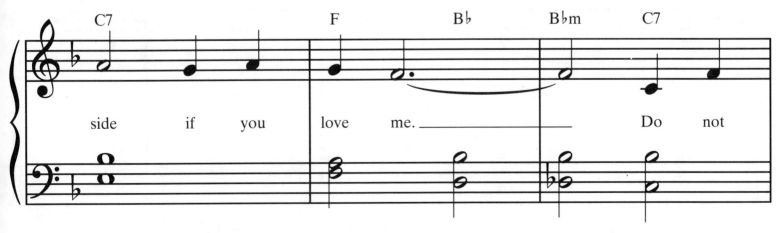

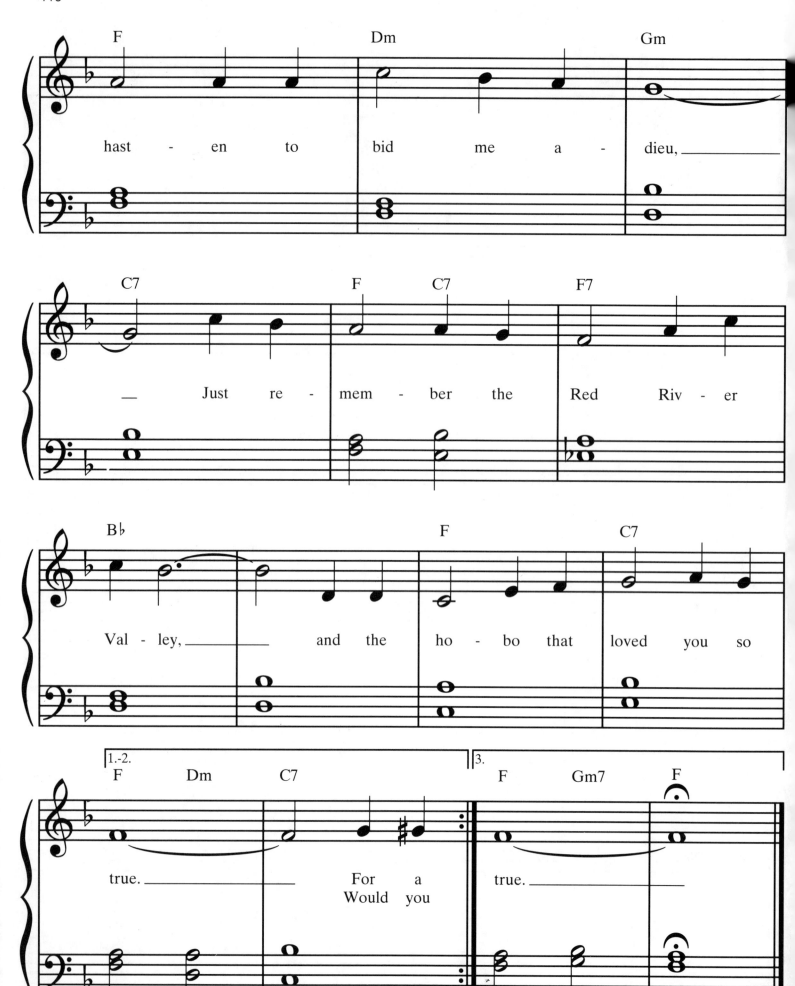

TEN LITTLE INDIANS

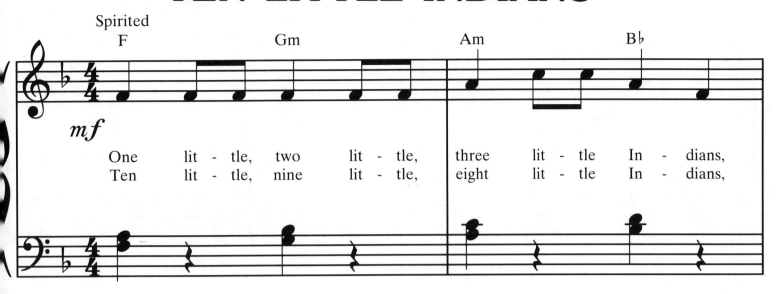

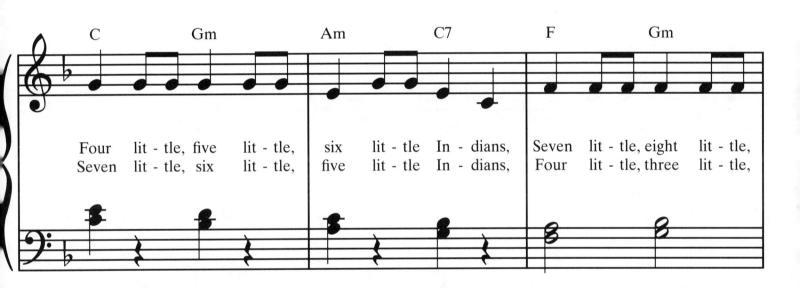

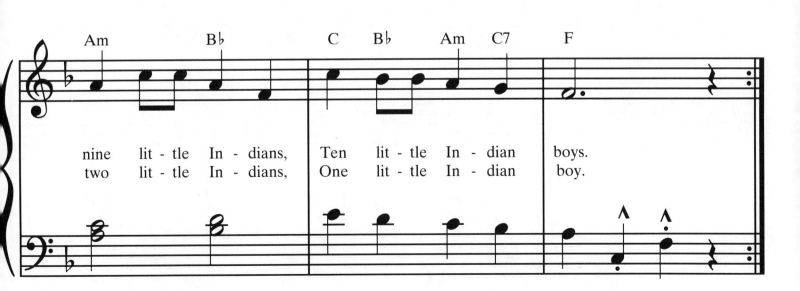

RING AROUND THE ROSIE

Brightly

Ring a - round the ros - y, a pock - et full of

po - sies; ash - es, ash - es, we all fall

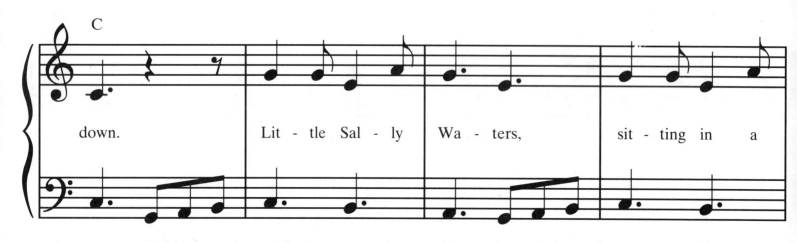

down. Lit - tle Sal - ly Wa - ters, sit - ting in a

sau - cer, weep - ing and a - moan - ing like a tur - tle

ROW, ROW, ROW YOUR BOAT

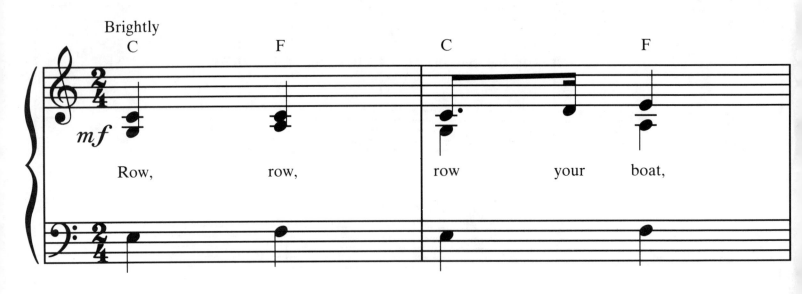

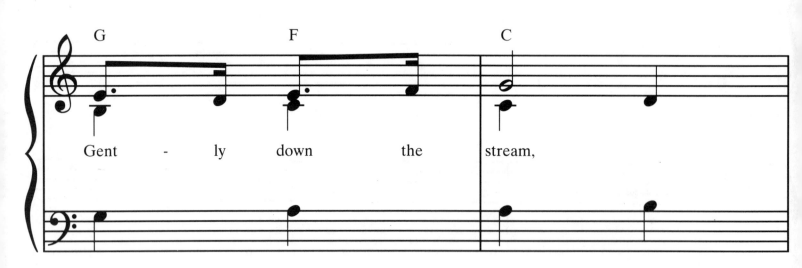

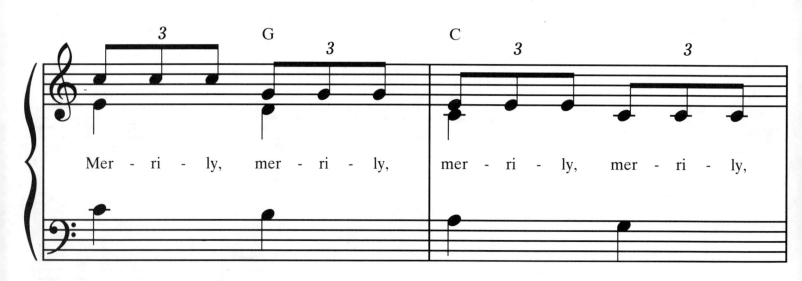

SCHOOL DAYS

123

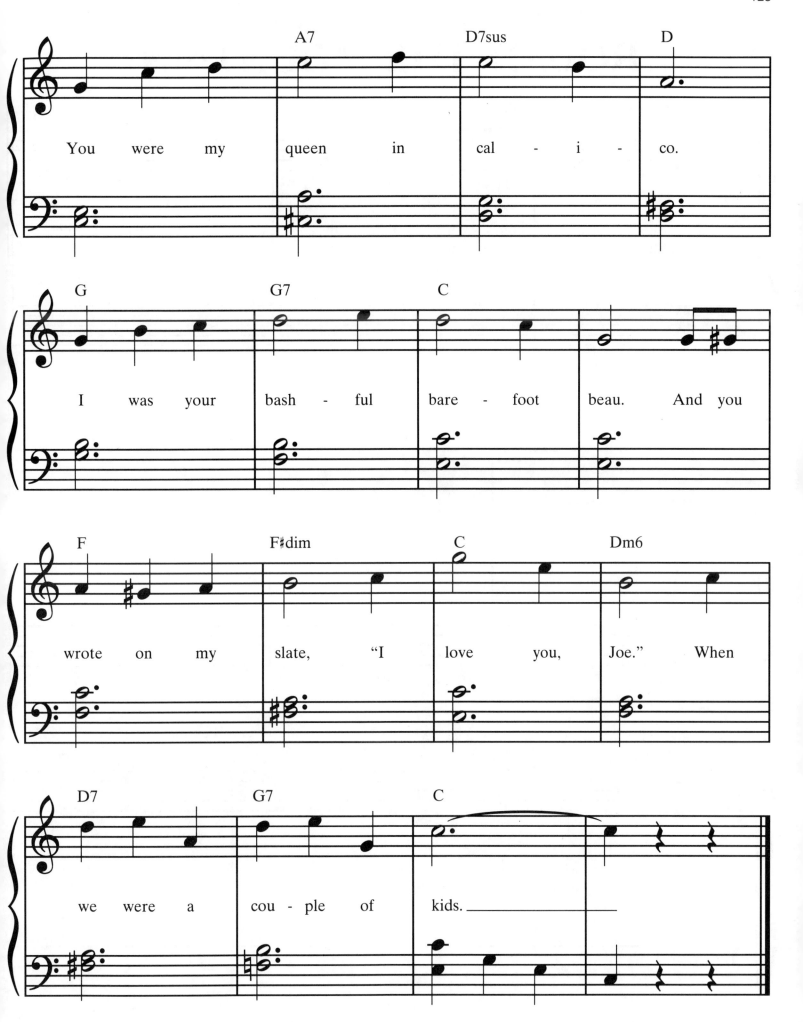

SHE'LL BE COMIN' 'ROUND THE MOUNTAIN

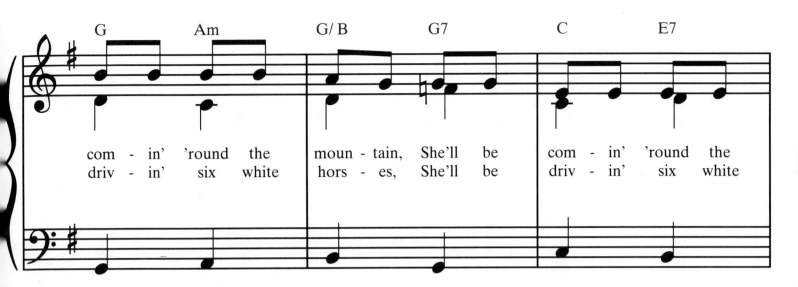

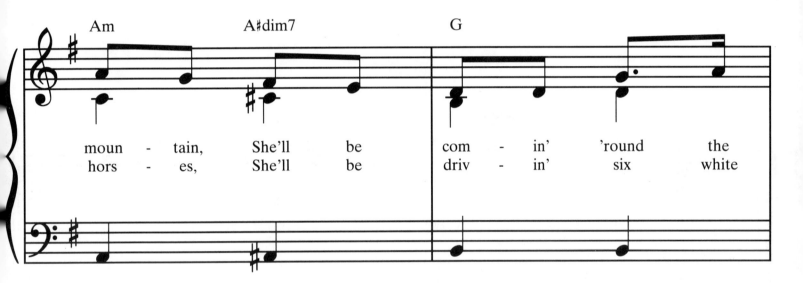

3. Oh, we'll all go to meet her when she comes,
   Oh, we'll all go to meet her when she comes,
   Oh, we'll all go to meet her,
   Oh, we'll all go to meet her,
   Oh, we'll all go to meet her when she comes.

4. We'll be singin' "Hallelujah" when she comes,
   We'll be singin' "Hallelujah" when she comes,
   We'll be singin' "Hallelujah,"
   We'll be singin' "Hallelujah,"
   We'll be singin' "Hallelujah" when she comes.

SKIP TO MY LOU

Lost my part-ner, what'll I do? Skip to my Lou, my dar - ling.

Lou, Lou, Skip to my Lou, Lou, Lou, Skip to my Lou,

Lou, Lou, Skip to my Lou, Skip to my Lou, my dar - ling.

2. I'll find another one, prettier than you,
   I'll find another one, prettier than you,
   I'll find another one, prettier than you,
   Skip to my Lou, my darling.

3. Little red wagon, painted blue.

4. Can't get a red bird, a blue bird'll do.

5. Cows in the meadow, moo, moo, moo.

6. Flies in the buttermilk, shoo, shoo, shoo.

SUPERCALIFRAGILISTIC-EXPIALIDOCIOUS

(From Walt Disney's "MARY POPPINS")

Words and Music by RICHARD M. SHERMAN
and ROBERT B. SHERMAN

THIS LAND IS YOUR LAND

Words and Music by WOODY GUTHRIE

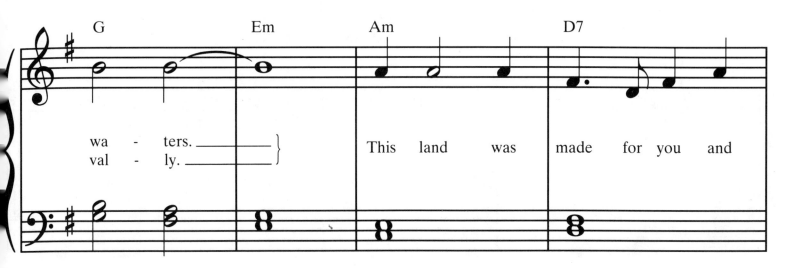

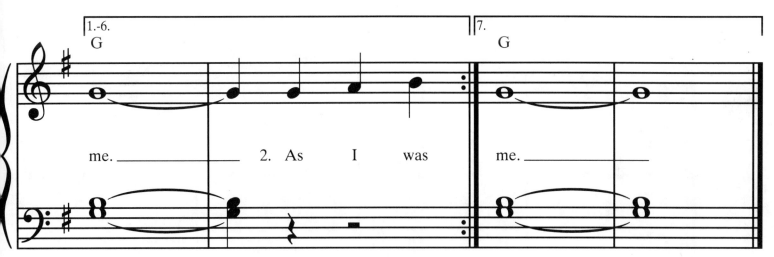

3. I've roamed and rambled and I followed my footsteps
   To the sparkling sands of her diamond deserts.
   And all around me a voice was sounding
   This land was made for you and me.

4. When the sun came shining, and I was strolling,
   And the wheat fields waving and the dust cloud rolling,
   As the fog was lifting a voice was chanting:
   This land was made for you and me.

5. As I went walking, I saw a sign there,
   And on the sign it said "No Trespassing."
   But on the other side it didn't say nothing,
   That side was made for you and me.

6. In the shadow of the steeple I saw my people,
   By the relief office I seen my people;
   As they stood there humgry, I stood there asking
   Is this land made for you and me?

7. Nobody living can ever stop me,
   As I go walking that freedom highway;
   Nobody living can ever make me turn back,
   This land was made for you and me.

THIS OLD MAN
(NICK NACK PADDY WACK)

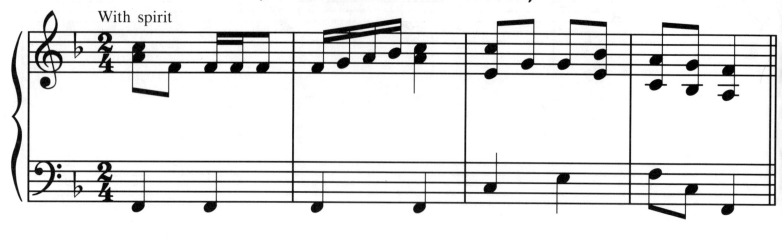

*Two . . . . on the shoe	*Six . . . . . on the sticks
*Three . . . on the tree	*Seven . . . up in heaven
*Four . . . . on the door	*Eight . . . on the gate
*Five . . . . on the hive	*Nine . . . . on the line

*Ten . . . . . once again

THREE BLIND MICE

TWINKLE, TWINKLE LITTLE STAR

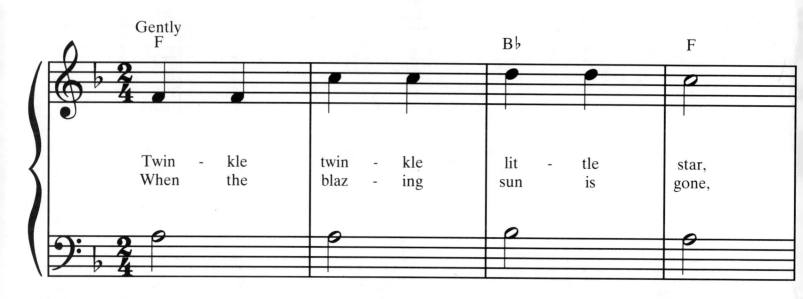

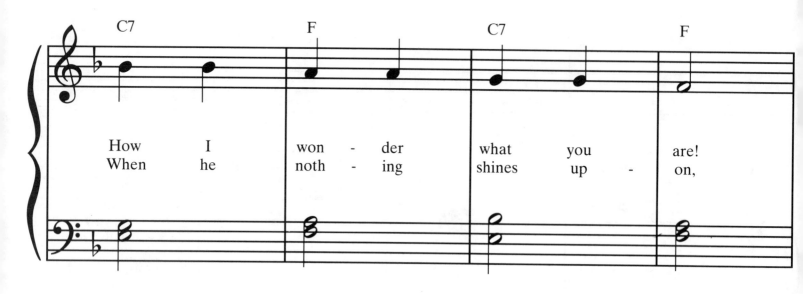

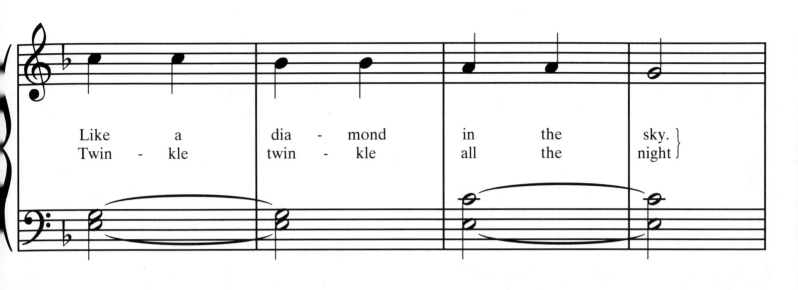

Like a diamond in the sky. }
Twin - kle twin - kle all the night }

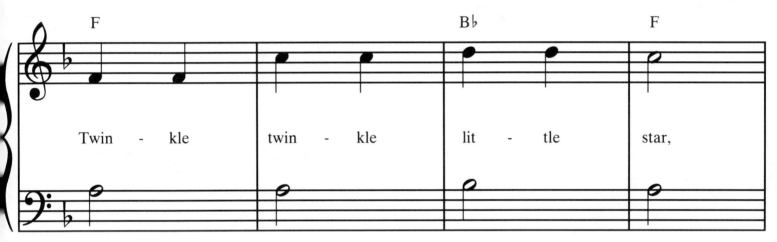

Twin - kle twin - kle lit - tle star,

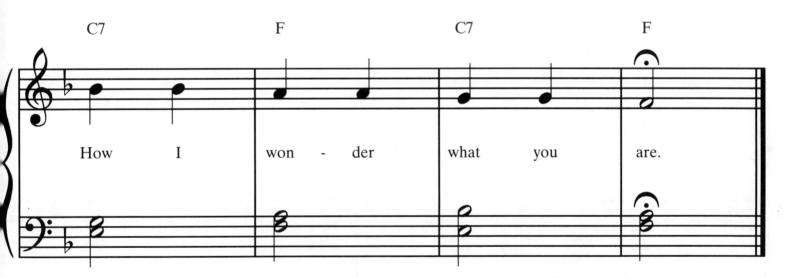

How I won - der what you are.

Parody

Starkle, starkle, little twink,
How I wonder what you think!
Up above the world so high,
Think you own the whole darn sky?
Starkle, starkle, little twink,
You're not so great,
That's what I think!

YANKEE DOODLE

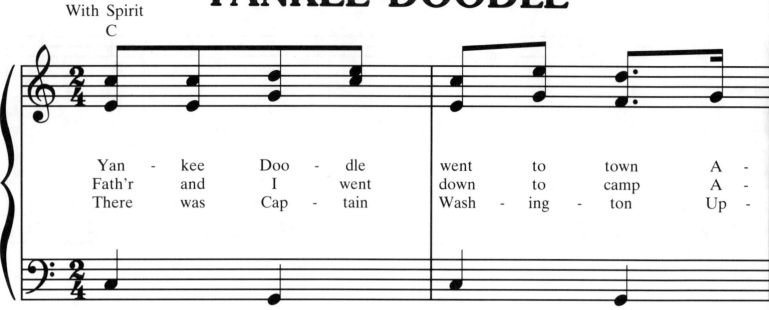

With Spirit

Yan - kee Doo - dle went to town A -
Fath'r and I went down to town camp A -
There was I Cap - tain Wash - ing - ton Up -

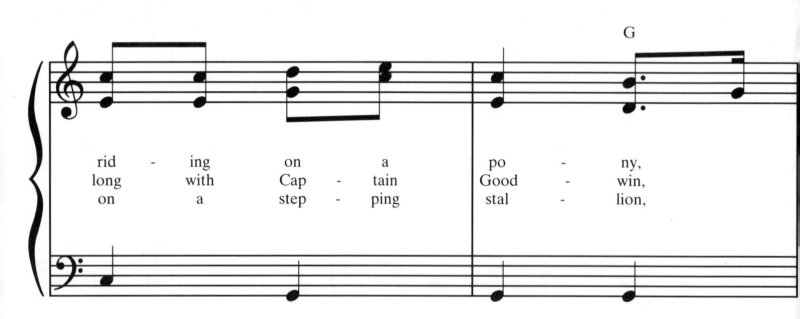

rid - ing on a po - ny,
long with Cap - tain Good - win,
on a step - ping stal - lion,

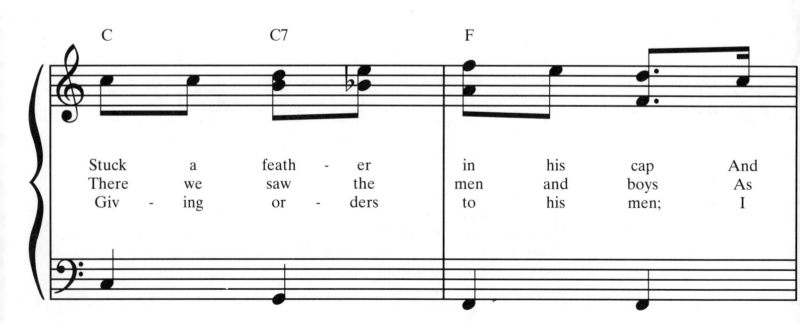

Stuck a feath - er in his cap And
There we saw the men and boys As
Giv - ing or - ders to his men; I

YELLOW SUBMARINE

Words and Music by
JOHN LENNON and PAUL McCARTNEY

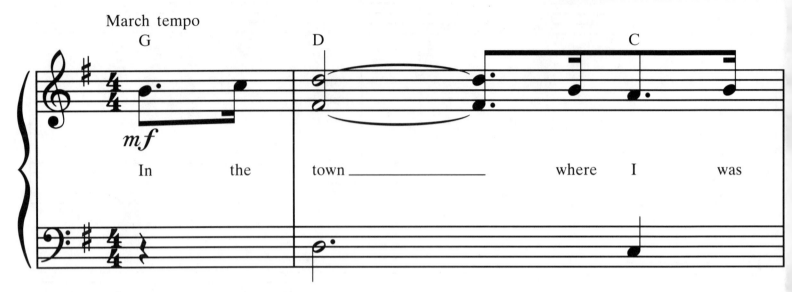

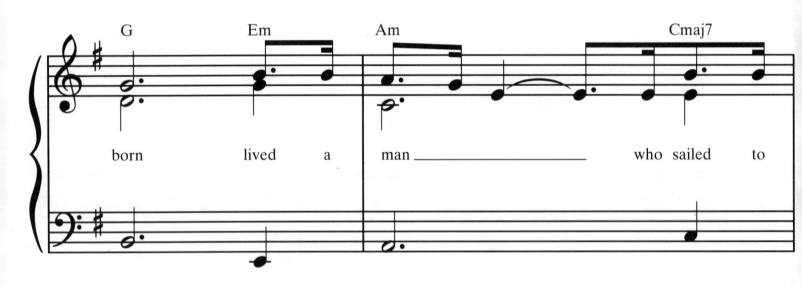

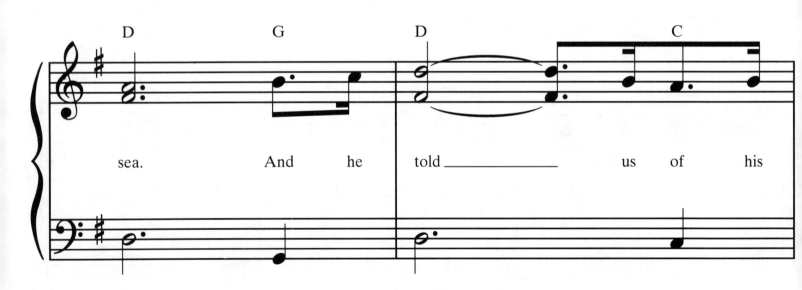

play:

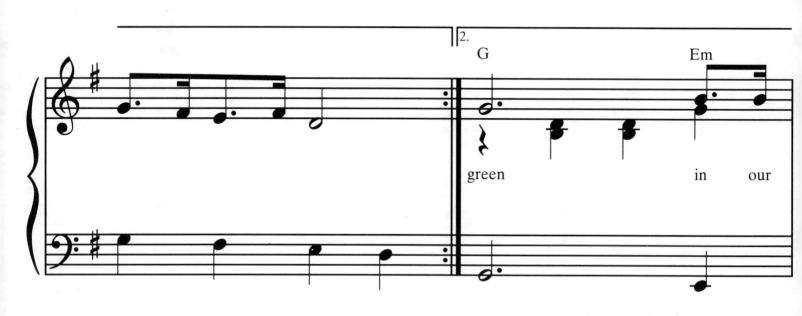

green   in our

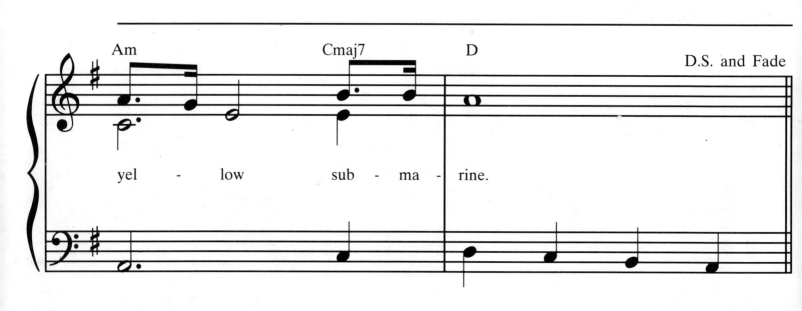

yel - low   sub - ma - rine.